DRAFTING:
TIPS AND TRICKS ON DRAWING AND DESIGNING HOUSE PLANS

BOB SYVANEN

The Globe Pequot Press

CHESTER, CONNECTICUT 06412

LIBRARY OF CONGRESS CATALOGING IN PUBLICATION DATA

SYVANEN, BOB, 1928-
    DRAFTING: TIPS AND TRICKS ON DRAWING AND DESIGNING HOUSE PLANS.

    I. ARCHITECTURE, DOMESTIC.. DESIGNS AND PLANS.
2. ARCHITECTURAL DRAWING. I. TITLE.
NA 7115.S97   720'.28'4   81-17344
ISBN 0-87106-501-0   AACR2

THIS BOOK WAS FIRST PRINTED BY THE AUTHOR IN 1981.
IF YOU HAVE ANY DRAFTING QUESTIONS, INCLUDE A STAMPED, SELF-ADDRESSED ENVELOPE AND SEND THEM TO:
BOB SYVANEN
179 UNDERPASS ROAD
BREWSTER, MASSACHUSETTS 02631

MANUFACTURED IN THE UNITED STATES OF AMERICA
FIRST EDITION / SIXTH PRINTING, 1989

IF YOU PLAN TO BUILD YOUR OWN HOUSE, THERE IS NO BETTER WAY TO START THAN BY DRAWING THE PLANS. THERE IS NO WAY TO SUCCEED AT A TASK WITHOUT GIVING IT A TRY. IT'S BEEN SAID THAT MOST OF US USE ABOUT FIVE PERCENT OF BODY- MIND POTENTIAL SO WITH A LITTLE EFFORT, SURELY WE CAN TAP THAT NINTY FIVE PERCENT. I HAVE FELT FOR SOME TIME NOW THAT ANYONE CAN DO ANYTHING, AND DESIGNING AND DRAWING YOUR OWN HOUSE PLANS IS JUST AN- OTHER ONE OF THOSE THINGS ANYONE CAN DO.

WITH THE HIGH COST OF EVERYTHING, HERE IS AN AREA WHERE A SUBSTAN- TIAL SAVING CAN BE MADE. A $40,000.00 HOUSE, DESIGNED AND DRAWN BY AN ARCHITECT WOULD COST FROM $1600.00 ON UP, DEPENDING ON DESIGN. (COMPLICAT- ED DESIGNS COST MORE). IF A DRAFTSMAN DRAWS THE PLANS, THEY WOULD COST FROM $800.00 ON UP. MOST ARCHITECTS WON'T TOUCH THE SMALL HOUSE. PLANS FOR A $90,000.00 HOUSE, ARCHITECT DESIGNED AND DRAWN, WOULD COST FROM $3200.00 ON UP AND DRAFTSMAN DRAWN, $1600.00 ON UP.

MOST PROBLEMS ARE OR SHOULD BE IRONED OUT ON PAPER BEFORE THE FIRST STICK IS CUT, IT'S CHEAPER THAT WAY. THE MORE KNOWLEGE YOU HAVE ON THE TOTAL SUBJECT, THE BETTER THE END PRODUCT WILL BE. IN FACT, I GOT INTO CARPENTRY THIRTY YEARS AGO SO THAT I WOULD BE A BETTER ARCHITECT. MY CARPENTRY BOOKS WOULD BE A HELP IN BOTH DESIGNING AND BUILDING. I ALWAYS KEEP THE CARPENTER IN MIND WHEN I DESIGN A HOUSE, BUT MY PRIMARY INTEREST IS THE CLIENT'S IDEAS. I TRY TO PUT ON PAPER WHAT THE CLIENT WANTS, NOT WHAT I WANT. I MERELY SUGGEST AND GUIDE. YOU, AS DESIGNER, CAN DO THE SAME WITH THAT INNER WISDOM WE ALL HAVE. VERY FEW HOUSES THAT ARE BUILT ARE ARCHITECT- DESIGNED, SO COME ON IN, THE WATERS FINE !

CONTENTS

INTRODUCTION _ 3

SECTION - 1 - EQUIPMENT _ 7

    DRAFTING BOARDS _ _ _ _ _ _ _ _ _ _ _ _ _ _ _ _ _ _ 8
    TRIANGLES _ _ _ _ _ _ _ _ _ _ _ _ _ _ _ _ _ _ _ 12
    SCALES _ _ _ _ _ _ _ _ _ _ _ _ _ _ _ _ _ _ _ 13
    PENCILS _ _ _ _ _ _ _ _ _ _ _ _ _ _ _ _ _ _ 14
    SHARPENERS _ _ _ _ _ _ _ _ _ _ _ _ _ _ _ _ 16
    TEMPLATES _ _ _ _ _ _ _ _ _ _ _ _ _ _ _ _ 17
    PAPER _ _ _ _ _ _ _ _ _ _ _ _ _ _ _ _ _ _ 19
    LIGHT TABLES _ _ _ _ _ _ _ _ _ _ _ _ _ _ _ _ 19

SECTION - 2 - DESIGN _ 21

    STYLES _ _ _ _ _ _ _ _ _ _ _ _ _ _ _ _ _ 22
    MEASURING TOOLS _ _ _ _ _ _ _ _ _ _ _ _ _ _ 25
    STAIRS _ _ _ _ _ _ _ _ _ _ _ _ _ _ _ _ 27
    CHIMNEYS _ _ _ _ _ _ _ _ _ _ _ _ _ _ _ 29
    HALLS & CLOSETS _ _ _ _ _ _ _ _ _ _ _ _ _ 30
    LOCATION _ _ _ _ _ _ _ _ _ _ _ _ _ _ _ 31
    QUICK TOPOGRAPHICAL SURVEY _ _ _ _ _ _ _ _ _ 33
    STRUCTURAL CONSIDERATIONS _ _ _ _ _ _ _ _ _ 34
    FIRST SKETCHES _ _ _ _ _ _ _ _ _ _ _ _ _ _ 40

SECTION - 3 - DRAFTING _ 45

    STEP - 1 _ _ _ _ _ _ _ _ _ _ _ _ _ _ _ _ 47
    STEP - 2 _ _ _ _ _ _ _ _ _ _ _ _ _ _ _ _ 48
    STEP - 3 _ _ _ _ _ _ _ _ _ _ _ _ _ _ _ _ 49
    STEP - 4 _ _ _ _ _ _ _ _ _ _ _ _ _ _ _ _ 50
    STEP - 5 _ _ _ _ _ _ _ _ _ _ _ _ _ _ _ _ 51
    STEP - 6 _ _ _ _ _ _ _ _ _ _ _ _ _ _ _ _ 53
    DIMENSION LINES _ _ _ _ _ _ _ _ _ _ _ _ _ 54
    STEP - 7 _ _ _ _ _ _ _ _ _ _ _ _ _ _ _ _ 57
    STEP - 8 _ _ _ _ _ _ _ _ _ _ _ _ _ _ _ _ 59

CONTENTS

STEP-9 --- 60
STEP-10 -- 61
ROOF TEXTURE --- 62
SIDEWALL TEXTURE --------------------------------------- 63
STEP-11 -- 65
DETAILS -- 66
SECTION -- 67
ELECTRICAL --- 68
PLOT PLAN -- 69
DOOR & WINDOW SCHEDULE --------------------------------- 70
ROOM SCHEDULE -- 71
LETTERING -- 72
SYMBOLS & ABBREVIATIONS -------------------------------- 75
TYPICAL FLOOR FRAMING PLAN ----------------------------- 77
TYPICAL ROOF FRAMING PLAN ------------------------------ 78
TYPICAL FLOOR PLAN ------------------------------------- 79
ROUGH DETAILS -- 80
LARGE SCALE DETAILS ------------------------------------ 83
REFINED DETAILS -- 87
PERSPECTIVES --- 88
LANDSCAPE PLAN --- 90
SMALL HOUSE PLAN --------------------------------------- 93-98
SMALL HOUSE PLAN --------------------------------------- 101-112

1 - EQUIPMENT

YOU CAN DRAW THE SAME SET OF PLANS WITH A T-SQUARE, TWO WOOD PENCILS A KITCHEN TABLE, AND A TRIANGLE AS YOU CAN WITH A FANCY TABLE, SEVEN TRIANGLES AND FIVE PENCILS. ONE SET WILL COST $15.00, THE OTHER $2500.00, BUT IT ALL BOILS DOWN TO HAND AND HEAD. THE BARE BONES EQUIPMENT AND A DESIRE ARE ALL YOU NEED FOR DRAWING YOUR OWN HOUSE PLANS.

EQUIPMENT

THE BARE BONES EQUIPMENT AND A DESIRE ARE ALL YOU REALLY NEED FOR DRAWING YOUR OWN HOUSE PLANS.

A TABLE WITH A STRAIGHT EDGE WILL WORK FINE FOR A DRAFTING BOARD.

TABLE THICKNESS

1 1/4"

2 1/2"

3/4"

ANY TABLE WILL WORK FINE, EVEN ONE WITHOUT A STRAIGHT EDGE. JUST MAKE UP A STRAIGHT EDGE FROM TWO PIECES OF WOOD, STRAIGHT PIECES WOULD HELP.

CLAMP IT TO THE END OF THE TABLE

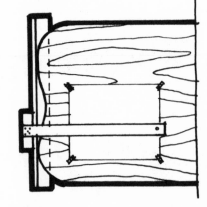

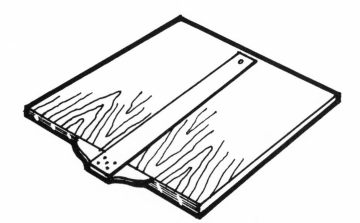

YOU CAN BUY A SMALL BOARD FOR ABOUT $25.00

OR YOU CAN MAKE ONE FROM 3/4" AC PLYWOOD, BOUGHT OR SCROUNGED. IF A T-SQUARE IS TO BE USED, ONE END HAS TO BE STRAIGHT AND SMOOTH. TO GET A NICE SLICK END, CEMENT A PIECE OF FORMICA ('KITCHEN COUNTER TOP MATERIAL) TO THE EDGE, IT IS TOO HARD TO USE FOR THE SURFACE. A SHEET OF HARD SURFACE PAPER OR $15.00 A SQUARE YARD VINYL (AVAILABLE AT DRAFT-ING SUPPLY STORES) MAKES A NICE WORK SURFACE. THE VINYL SURFACE IS SOFT ENOUGH SO THAT PENCIL WORK WONT TEAR EVEN THIN TRACING PAPER. IT'S EASY TO CLEAN AND LASTS FOREVER. ATTACH IT TO THE BOARD WITH 1" DOUBLE COATED TAPE.

A SOLID CORE DOOR MAKES A BEAUTIFUL TABLE (VERY HEAVY, BUT A NICE SURFACE). THERE ARE PLENTY OF USED DOORS AT BUILDING SALVAGE YARDS. A HOLLOW CORE DOOR WILL DO IF YOU CHOOSE CAREFULLY. THE OLD-ER HOLLOW CORE DOORS HAVE A BETTER SURFACE THAN THE NEW ONES. THE SMOOTHER THE SURFACE THE FEWER PROBLEMS YOU WILL HAVE IN KEEP-ING THE DRAWINGS CLEAN. THE LITTLE BUMPS GET RUBBED BY THE TOOLS, SMUDGING THE DRAWING. DOORS FOR TOPS WILL BE ABOUT 3 FEET BY 7 FEET. I WOULDN'T GO OVER 2 FEET BY 3 FEET WITH 3/4" PLYWOOD UNLESS IT IS REINFORCED UNDERNEATH TO PREVENT SAG AND WARP. SAND THE SURFACE AND BRUSH IT CLEAN BEFORE PUTTING PAPER OR VINYL ON. ANY SMALL PARTICLES WILL CAUSE BUMPS ON THE SURFACE AND THESE WILL CAUSE SMUDGES ON THE DRAWINGS.

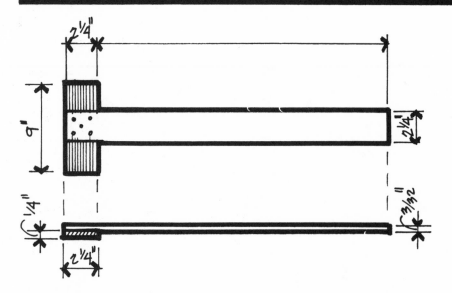

SINCE THE PARALLEL STRAIGHT EDGE WAS REFINED, THE T-SQUARE ISN'T USED MUCH THESE DAYS, BUT IT STILL WILL DO A GOOD JOB. YOU CAN MAKE ONE, BUT IT IS HARDLY WORTH WHILE WHEN A SMALL WOOD ONE COSTS BUT A FEW BUCKS, EVEN A GOOD ONE A FEW DOLLARS MORE. IF YOU MAKE ONE, TRY TO MAKE THE BLADE PERPENDICULAR TO THE HEAD, BUT DON'T BE CONCERNED IF IT IS NOT; IT WILL STILL SLIDE UP AND DOWN PARALLEL. JUST BE SURE THE HEAD IS FIRMLY ANCHORED TO THE BLADE WITH 5 WOOD SCREWS.

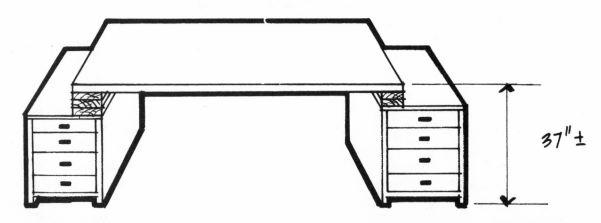

THE HEIGHT OF THE BOARD IS A MATTER OF PERSONAL PREFERENCE; REMEMBER YOU MIGHT WANT TO WORK BOTH SITTING AND STANDING. MY BOARD IS 37" HIGH AND FLAT, I DON'T LIKE TO CHASE PENCILS. MOST PEOPLE LIKE THE BOARD RAISED A FEW INCHES ON THE FAR EDGE. IF THE BOARD IS HIGH (37"), THEN YOU MUST SIT ON A HIGH STOOL, 30" IN MY CASE. TABLE HEIGHT (29") IS FINE TO WORK AT, BUT ONLY SITTING. THE BOARD CAN BE SUPPORTED ON HORSES MADE FOR THE JOB, OR BLOCKED UP ON CABINETS, DRESSERS, OR BOXES.

IF PLYWOOD IS USED, A WOOD SUB-FRAME SHOULD BE BUILT AND THEN THE WHOLE BUSINESS SUPPORTED.

THERE IS A NICE LITTLE 18"x24" BOARD WITH A PARALLEL STRAIGHT EDGE FOR ABOUT $35.00. THE LARGEST ONE I KNOW OF IS 23"x31" AND THE SMALLEST IS 12"x17".

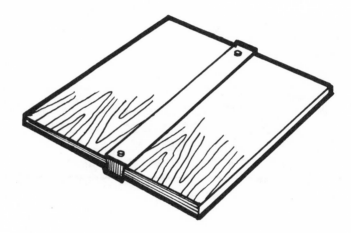

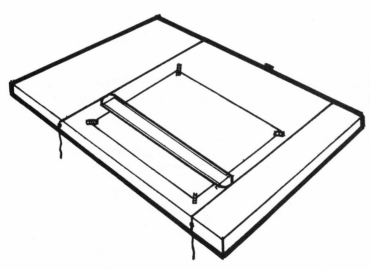

PARALLEL STRAIGHT EDGES COME IN SIZES 36", 48", 54", 60", 72". I LIKE THE 48" SIZE, A NICE IN-BETWEEN LENGTH. WITH THE PARALLEL STRAIGHT EDGE YOU DON'T HAVE TO HOLD THE STRAIGHT EDGE AND TRIANGLE AS YOU WOULD WITH THE T-SQUARE. AND IT IS ALWAYS PARALLEL NO MATTER WHERE YOU PUSH IT ON THE BOARD. BE SURE THE BOARD IS LONGER THAN THE STRAIGHT EDGE.

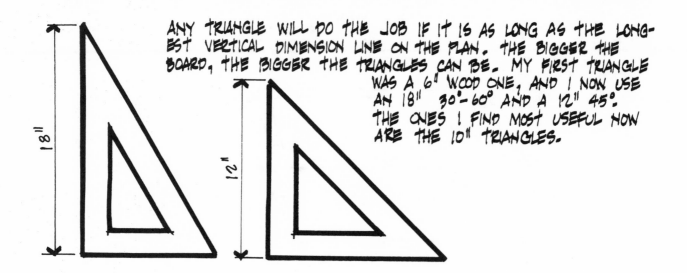

ANY TRIANGLE WILL DO THE JOB IF IT IS AS LONG AS THE LONG-EST VERTICAL DIMENSION LINE ON THE PLAN. THE BIGGER THE BOARD, THE BIGGER THE TRIANGLES CAN BE. MY FIRST TRIANGLE WAS A 6" WOOD ONE, AND I NOW USE AN 18" 30°-60° AND A 12" 45°. THE ONES I FIND MOST USEFUL NOW ARE THE 10" TRIANGLES.

A REALLY GREAT TRIANGLE IS THE 10" ADJUSTABLE THAT COMES IN TWO STYLES. ONE MEASURES DEGREES AND THE OTHER ROOF PITCHES; EITHER WILL DO, BUT SINCE MY ROOF PITCH ONE VANISHED I CANNOT LOCATE ANOTHER. A GOOD REASON TO SCRATCH YOUR INITIALS ON TOOLS!

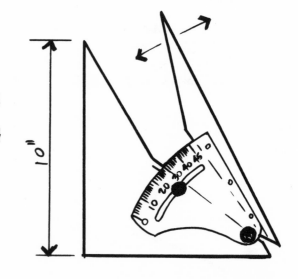

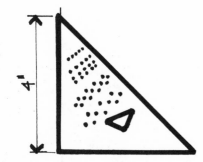

ANOTHER GOOD TRIANGLE IS THE 45 LETTERING GUIDE. THERE IS A 6" MODEL, BUT I FIND THE 4" K&E 1859-C-4 MODEL GOOD ENOUGH.

THE AMES LETTERING GUIDE IS PROBABLY THE MOST COMMON GUIDE AROUND, BUT TAKE YOUR PICK.

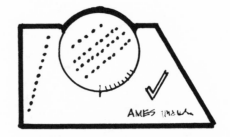

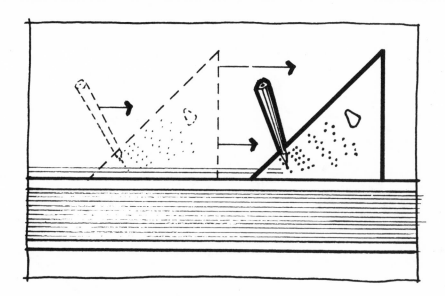

IT IS PRETTY OBVIOUS HOW THE LETTERING GUIDES ARE USED - THE PENCIL POINT IS PUT INTO A HOLE OF YOUR CHOICE AND THEN YOU SLIDE THE TRIANGLE, ALONG THE STRAIGHT EDGE, WITH THE PENCIL. BRING THE WHOLE BUSINESS BACK, PUT THE POINT IN A HOLE THAT WILL GIVE THE SPACING DESIRED, AND THEN SLIDE AGAIN. PESTO, TWO PARALLEL LINES! ONE CAUTION; THE GUIDES GET DIRTY. KEEP THEM CLEAN AND USE ONLY FOR LETTERING WORK OR ELSE YOU WILL FIND THE DRAWING WILL GET MESSY.

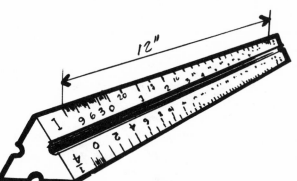

HOUSE PLANS DON'T HAVE TO BE DRAWN SUPER ACCURATELY AS LONG AS THE NUMBERS ARE CORRECT. I USED A PLAIN WOOD RULER WITH 1/16" INCREMENTS WHEN I STARTED. THE 12 INCH TRIANGULAR SCALE IS THE MOST FAMILIAR AND AN INEXPENSIVE WOOD SCALE WILL MEASURE THE SAME AS AN EXPENSIVE ONE, BUT NOT AS EASY ON THE EYES.

THIS 6" FLAT SCALE HAS 8 GRADUATIONS, 4 ON THE TOP AND 4 ON THE BOTTOM.

THIS FLAT SCALE HAS 4 GRADUATIONS AND THEY ARE ALL VISIBLE ON THE TOP. THE TRIANGLE SCALES ALWAYS SEEM TO HAVE THE SCALE YOU NEED ON THE BOTTOM.

EQUIPMENT

IN THE EARLY DAYS EVERYTHING WAS INKED AFTER FIRST DRAWING IN PENCIL. WHAT A DRAG! NOW ALL WE NEED IS GOOD PENCIL WORK AND WOOD PENCILS WORK FINE.

USE ANY SHARP TOOL TO CUT AWAY THE WOOD LEAVING ABOUT ¾" OF LEAD EXPOSED. ▬

THE LEAD IS THEN SHARPENED BY RUBBING THE TIP ON A PIECE OF SANDPAPER. WIPE THE DUST OFF WHEN FINISHED.

THE MECHANICAL PENCIL SAVES A LOT OF TIME. THE ONE MOST USED IS A PENCIL SHAPED METAL TUBE WITH A CHUCK AT THE POINT END THAT HOLDS ONE LONG PIECE OF LEAD. THE LEAD IS ADVANCED BY PRESSING THE REAR OF THE PENCIL WITH THE THUMB, OPENING THE CHUCK. THE LEAD IS FREE TO SLIDE OUT AS FAR AS NEEDED. THE TIP IS INSERTED INTO A PENCIL SHARPENER OR RUBBED ON A PIECE OF SANDPAPER. I USE THIS STYLE PENCIL WITH AN "H" OR "F" LEAD FOR HEAVY LINE WORK AND HEAVY LETTER-ING.

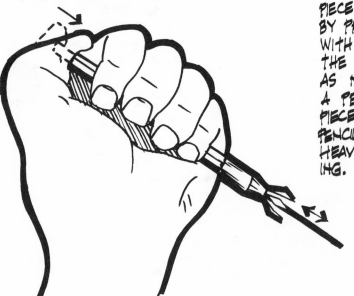

I THINK THE BEST PENCIL TO COME DOWN THE PIKE IS THE 5 MM MICRO LEAD. NOT EVERYONE CAN USE THIS PENCIL WITHOUT CONSTANTLY BREAKING THE LEADS. THIS PENCIL MUST BE HELD NEARLY VERTICAL AND WITH A GOOD TOUCH. THE BARREL IS LOADED WITH A DOZEN LEADS AND A CLICK OF THE THUMB, SIMILAR TO A BALL POINT PEN, WILL ADVANCE THE LEAD AND YOU ARE READY FOR WORK. IT'S CLEAN AND IT'S QUICK. YOU CAN'T BEAT IT FOR LAYOUT WORK WHERE YOU NEED A LIGHT TOUCH. THE LEADS COME IN ALL THE STANDARD DEGREES. I FIND THE 2H GOOD FOR LAYOUT AND THE H OR F GOOD FOR LETTERING.

THE MICRO LEADS NEED NO SHARPENING, ALL OTHERS NEED AT LEAST A PIECE OF SANDPAPER. THERE IS A 4" WOOD STICK WITH A DOZEN PIECES OF SANDPAPER GLUED ON MADE JUST FOR SHARPENING LEADS.

THERE IS A NEAT LITTLE K&E SHARPENER. MIGHT BE HARD TO FIND, BUT THERE ARE SIMILAR ONES.

JUST INSERT THE TIP AND TWIST

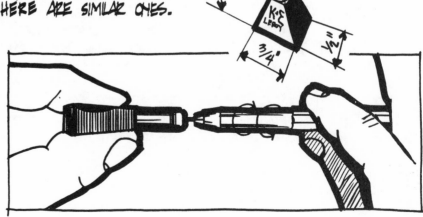

EQUIPMENT

YOU CAN GO TO THE BIGGER METAL SHARPENERS.

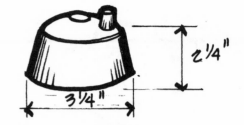

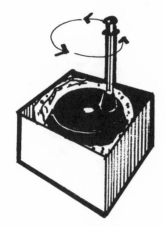

I KEEP THE ONE I HAVE IN ITS BOX. SURROUND IT WITH FOAM TO KEEP IT STEADY AND TO CLEAN THE POINT AFTER SHARPENING.

KOH-I-NOR MAKES A NICE PLASTIC SHARPENER THAT CLAMPS TO THE BOARD.

RWS

ALL OF THESE SHARPENERS CREATE A LOT OF DUST, SO BE CAREFUL. WIPE THE LEAD POINTS AND BRUSH OFF THE DRAWING FREQUENTLY, ESPECIALLY AFTER ERASING. ERASER PARTICLES ARE DIRTY AND THEY WILL SMUDGE THE DRAWINGS.

THERE IS A 4" CLOTH BAG, FILLED WITH CLEAN GROUND-UP ERASER PARTICLES, THAT YOU PAT ON THE DRAWING. THIS LEAVES SALT GRAIN SIZE BITS OF ERASER THAT THE TOOLS RIDE ON.

A GOOD WAY TO KEEP DRAWINGS CLEAN IS TO COVER EVERYTHING EXCEPT THE AREA BEING WORKED ON. ANY CLEAN PAPER WILL DO, BUT DO TAPE IT DOWN. THIS IS PARTICULARLY GOOD FOR LARGE DRAWING WITH MUCH WORK ON IT.

A THIN METAL ERASING SHIELD IS AN INEXPENSIVE ITEM WORTH HAVING.

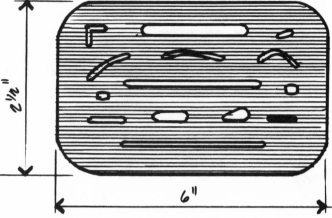

2½"

6"

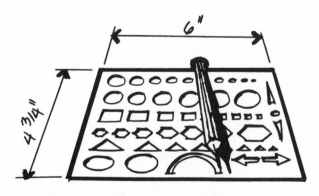

IT LETS YOU ERASE AN AREA WITHOUT DISTURBING WHAT IS AROUND IT. IT ALSO CLEANS THE ERASER.

THERE ARE THREE BASIC ERASERS: THE VINYL, THE GUM, AND THE RUBBER. THE OLD FASHIONED "SOAP" OR GUM ERASER IS STILL A GOOD ONE, BUT THE VINYL IS THE MOST POPULAR NOW. THE "PINK PEARL" RUBBER ERASER HAS BEEN AROUND A LONG TIME AND IT TOO IS A GOOD ERASER.

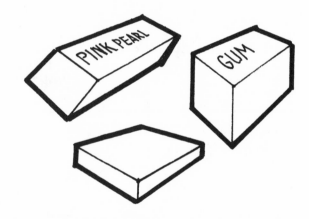

6"

4 3/4"

I HAVE A COUPLE OF FANCY COMPASSES THAT I RARELY USE SINCE ACQUIRING CIRCLE TEMPLATES. THE ONE MOST USED IS A 4"X6" COMBINATION CIRCLE, SQUARE, HEX, TRIANGLE TEMPLATE. A GOOD BASIC TEMPLATE. THERE IS ALSO A LARGE CIRCLE TEMPLATE WITH RADIUSES FROM 1/16" TO 3".

PLUMBING FIXTURE TEMPLATES, SOMETIMES AVAILABLE FROM PLUMBING SUPPLY STORES, BUT MORE EASILY PURCHASED AT DRAFTING SUPPLY STORES, ARE HANDY TOOLS. THERE ARE TEMPLATES FOR JUST ABOUT ANYTHING YOU NEED TO DRAW AND THEY ARE VERY HELPFUL., BUT NOT NECESSARY.

EQUIPMENT

3/4" WIDE MASKING TAPE IS A NICE SIZE TO USE FOR HOLDING DRAWINGS ON THE BOARD. BE SURE TO USE DRAFTING MASKING TAPE; IT'S NOT AS STICKY AS THE OTHER TAPES. YOU WILL HAVE LESS TROUBLE PEELING IT OFF. SCOTCH TAPE NO. 230 IS A DRAFTING MASKING TAPE.

GOOD LIGHTING HELPS TO MAKE THE WORK EASIER ESPECIALLY AS THE EYES GET OLDER. ANY LIGHT SHOULD COME FROM THE UPPER LEFT, FOR RIGHTIES, UPPER RIGHT FOR LEFTIES. JUST BE SURE THE STRAIGHT EDGE OR TRIANGLE DOES NOT CAST A SHADOW ON THE LINE BEING DRAWN. THE BEST LAMP IS A CLAMP-ON ADJUSTABLE THAT LETS YOU PUT THE LIGHT JUST WHERE IT IS NEEDED.

A RIGHT HANDED PERSON HOLDS THE TRIANGLE WITH THE LEFT HAND AND REACHES ACROSS WITH THE RIGHT TO DRAW A VERTICAL LINE.

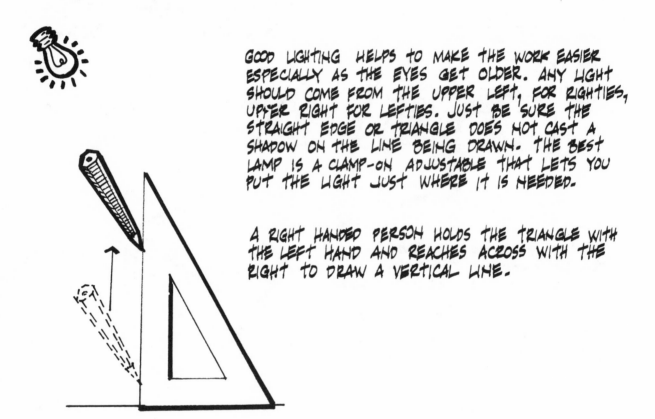

A POCKET CALCULATOR IS A TOOL THAT IS NOT NECESSARY, BUT IT SURE HELPS ME. IT NOT ONLY SAVES TIME AND HELPS AVOID ERRORS, IT MAKES MATH ALMOST FUN.

TRACING PAPER IS PRETTY MUCH A MATTER OF PREFERENCE. ANY TRACING PAPER WILL BE FINE, BUT SOME ARE BETTER THAN OTHERS. FOR THE SERIOUS DRAFTS-MAN I LIKE CLEARPRINT 1000H, K&E CRYSTALENE OR K&E ALBANENE MEDIUM WEIGHT. ALL CAN BE PURCHASED BY THE ROLL OR SHEET. THESE PAPERS HAVE A "TOOTH" OR TEXTURE THAT SUITS MY HAND AND PENCILS. IF XEROX IS USED FOR PRINTS, THEN ANY KIND OF PAPER WILL DO, BUT TRACING PAPER IS PREFERRED FOR EASE OF TRACING THE DIFFERENT FLOOR PLANS. IF YOU HAVE A LIGHT TABLE THEN ANYTHING GOES.

I WOULD NOT BE WITHOUT A ROLL OF THIN YELLOW TRACING PAPER (THE TALKING PAPER) AND FELT TIP PENS. 14" AND 18" WIDE BY 50 YARDS I FIND THE MOST USEFUL AND AT $5.00 A ROLL - WELL WORTH IT! THE CHOICE OF FELT TIP DEPENDS ON WHAT WORKS BEST FOR YOU. SOME PEOPLE LIKE WORKING WITH FINE LINES WHILE OTHERS PREFER HEAVY LINES.

A LIGHT TABLE CAN BE VERY EXPENSIVE OR YOU CAN MAKE A WOOD FRAME BOX WITH A FEW LIGHT SOCKETS INSIDE AND A PIECE OF 3/16" OR 1/4" FROSTED GLASS FOR A WORK SURFACE. A PIECE OF 1/4" PLATE GLASS ON A COUPLE OF BOOKS AT EACH CORNER AND A LIGHT DIRECTED UNDER IS AN EFFECTIVE LIGHT TABLE. THERE IS A LOT OF HEAT GENERATED PARTICULARLY IF THE LIGHTS ARE ENCLOSED, SO VENTILATE.

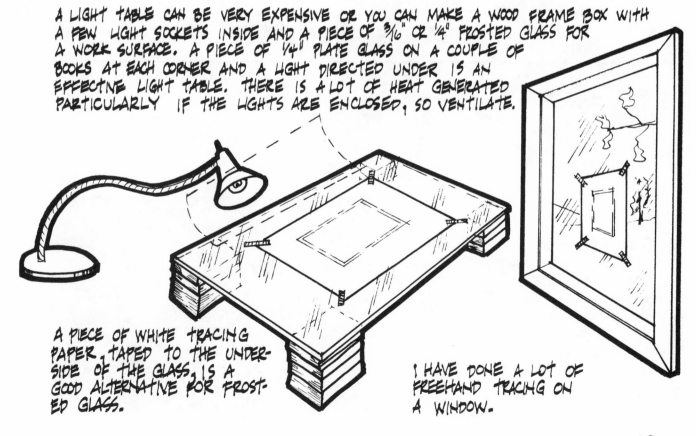

A PIECE OF WHITE TRACING PAPER, TAPED TO THE UNDER-SIDE OF THE GLASS, IS A GOOD ALTERNATIVE FOR FROST-ED GLASS.

I HAVE DONE A LOT OF FREEHAND TRACING ON A WINDOW.

EQUIPMENT

CLEAN ALL TRIANGLES, STRAIGHT EDGES, SCALES, TEMPLATES AND TABLE TOPS BEFORE THEY GET TOO DIRTY. IT WILL GO A LONG WAY TOWARDS KEEPING DRAWINGS CLEAN. CLEAN DRAWINGS REPRODUCE SHARPER AND THEREFORE ARE EASIER TO READ.

THESE ARE SOME BASIC TOOLS. THE DRAFTING BOARD IS A 24" X 30" X 3/4" PIECE OF PINE FACED PLYWOOD COVERED WITH VINYL. THE SURFACE UNDER THE VINYL SHOULD BE SMOOTH OR EVERY BUMP WILL SHOW.

A FEW MORE TOOLS TO MAKE THE WORK EASIER.

THE NEXT STEP UP. THIS BOARD IS A 3'-0" X 6'-8" SOLID CORE DOOR. THE VINYL COVERING OVER THE BIRCH DOOR MAKES FOR A NICE SMOOTH SURFACE.

2-DESIGN

MOST HOUSES ARE OWNER OR BUILDER-DESIGNED, SO IF YOU ARE AN OWNER OR BUILDER YOU CAN DESIGN YOUR HOUSE. WE ALL KNOW A GOOD HOUSE WHEN WE SEE IT. WE ALSO KNOW OUR LIMITATIONS, OR DO WE SET OUR LIMITS?

AS WE ENTER THE 80's KEEP IN MIND WHAT THE "EXPERTS" ARE SAYING IN LIGHT OF THE HIGH COST OF CONSTRUCTION AND FUEL:

1. MORE ENERGY-EFFICIENT CONSTRUCTION.

2. FEWER AND SMALLER BEDROOMS.

3. NO FAMILY ROOMS.

4. SUMMER AND WINTER LIVING (CLOSE OFF PART OF THE HOUSE TO CONSERVE FUEL).

5. TWO GENERATIONS UNDER ONE ROOF.

THE DESIGN INFORMATION THAT FOLLOWS IS NOT VERY SOPHISTICATED, JUST VERY BASIC CONSIDERATIONS. THINGS LIKE FEELINGS, OBSERVATION, STAIRWAYS, CHIMNEYS, ETC. YOU CAN EXPAND FROM THESE BASICS AS YOUR NEEDS AND DESIRES DICTATE.

DESIGN

THE FIRST CONSIDERATION IN DESIGNING YOUR HOUSE IS TO REALIZE THAT YOU CAN DO IT. AFTER ALL, YOU DESIGN EVERY DAY WHEN DRESSING....

ARRANGING FURNITURE, FLOWERS, AND DRAPES.

YOU LOOK AT A HOUSE AND SOMETHING CLICKS— IT'S GOOD LOOKING OR IT'S AWFUL. THE ROOF ANGLE IS WRONG, THE CHIMNEY IS TOO THIN. TALK TO YOURSELF, CALL ON THAT INNER WISDOM WE ALL HAVE. TAKE PLENTY OF NOTES.

DON'T YOU THINK THE PIANO IN THE OTHER CORNER WOULD LOOK BETTER, MARY ?

NEXT, CONSIDER THE NEED, WANTS AND LIFE STYLE. TO START SMALL BECAUSE POCKET- BOOK AND NEED ARE SMALL AND ADD AS THEY CHANGE IS A GOOD WAY TO GO. WHAT WE THOUGHT TODAY FREQUENTLY CHANGES TOMORROW.

ADD ANOTHER ROOM JOE, THE RABBIT DIED.

NO MATTER WHAT YOU DESIGN, HALF THE PEOPLE WILL LOVE IT AND THE OTHER HALF HATE IT.

DESIGN

IF YOU SEE A HOUSE YOU LIKE DON'T BE AFRAID TO COPY IT OR USE PARTS IN YOUR OWN DESIGN. ALL THE EARLY CAVES WERE PRETTY MUCH ALIKE.

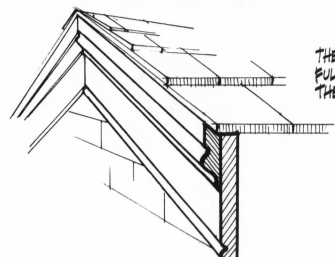

THE EARLY CAPE COD HOUSES WERE EITHER FULL CAPE, HALF CAPE, OR SALT BOX. THE VARIATIONS WERE IN THE ADDITIONS AND THE TRIM.

WHEN YOU SEE A NICE HOUSE, TAKE PICTURES AND MEASURE- MENTS. TALK TO THE OWNERS. THEY WILL BE FLATTERED THAT YOU LIKE THEIR HOUSE.

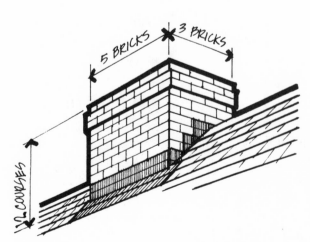

COUNT THE BRICKS OF A CHIMNEY YOU LIKE TO DETERMINE ITS SIZE. A BRICK IS 2" THICK BY 4" WIDE BY 8" LONG. MAKE NOTE OF THE ROOF SIZE AND PITCH. THAT SAME CHIMNEY MIGHT NOT LOOK GOOD ON A DIFFERENT ROOF.

TRY TO CARRY A TAPE MEASURE AND POCKET CALCULATOR.

YOU MIGHT SEE A PIECE OF TRIM YOU LIKE. OR MAYBE IT WOULD LOOK BETTER THINNER. TAKE NOTES; YOU WILL FILL A BOOK BEFORE YOU KNOW IT.

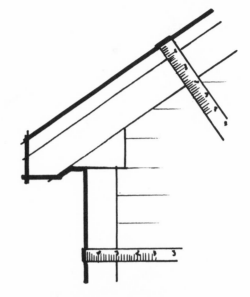

IF YOU DON'T HAVE A TAPE MEASURE WITH YOU, USE WHAT YOU DO HAVE, YOUR BODY. KNOW YOUR STRIDE (ABOUT 36")....

3'- 6"

2'- 6"

3'- 0"

3'- 0" ?

POTENTIAL BASKET- BALL STAR.

BIG DOESN'T AL- WAYS MEAN A LONG STRIDE.

SOME WOMEN HAVE VERY LONG LEGS.

DON'T STRETCH IT, THE STRIDE WILL BE INCONSISTENT.

DESIGN

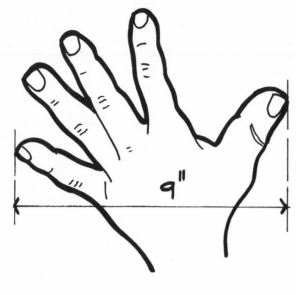

KNOW YOUR HAND....

....THIS IS HANDY

9"

SO IS THIS.....

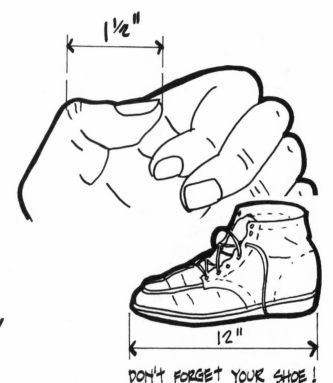

1 ½"

1"

12"

DON'T FORGET YOUR SHOE!

WHEN IN A ROOM THAT FEELS GOOD AND COMFORT-
ABLE, TRY TO FIGURE WHY. IS IT THE CEIL-
ING HEIGHT, LENGTH TO WIDTH RATIO OF THE
ROOM, WINDOW SIZES AND SPACES? MEASURE
ALL THE CONTRIBUTING FACTORS. HOW FAR IS
YOUR HAND FROM THE CEILING WHEN RAISED?
COUNT FLOOR TILES AND HERE IS A GOOD TIME
TO USE YOUR HAND SPAN. TILES ARE EITHER
9" OR 12". TAKE NOTES ABOUT THINGS THAT
DON'T PLEASE YOU TOO; WE LEARN FROM GOOD
AND BAD.

WHAT A NICE FEEL
TO THIS ROOM.

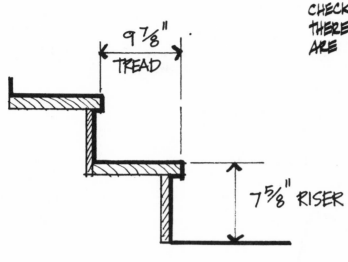

9⅞" TREAD

7⅝" RISER

CHECK THE RISE AND TREAD ON STAIRS. THERE IS AN IDEAL OR AVERAGE, BUT ARE YOU AVERAGE?

$$9\tfrac{7}{8}"$$
$$+\ 7\tfrac{5}{8}"$$
$$\overline{17\tfrac{1}{2}"}$$ THIS IS THE IDEAL TOTAL OF RISE AND TREAD.

AVAILABLE SPACE CONTROLS SHAPE OF STAIRWAYS....

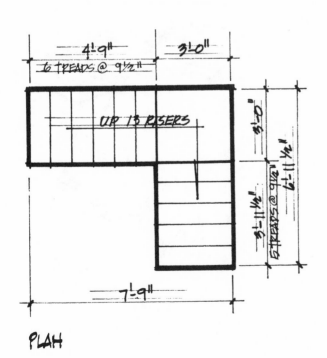

4'-9"   3'-0"
6 TREADS @ 9½"

UP 13 RISERS

3'-0"

6'-11½"
3'-11½"
6 TREADS @ 9½"

7'-9"

PLAN

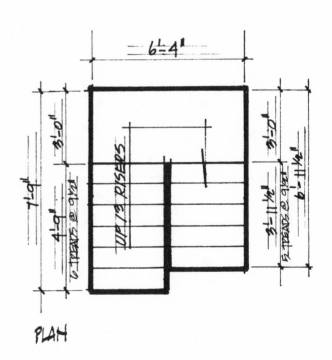

6'-4"

3'-0"

3'-0"

7'-0"
4'-9"
6 TREADS @ 9½"

UP 13 RISERS

6'-11½"
3'-11½"
6 TREADS @ 9½"

PLAN

CODE AND COMFORT DETERMINE SIZE.

DESIGN

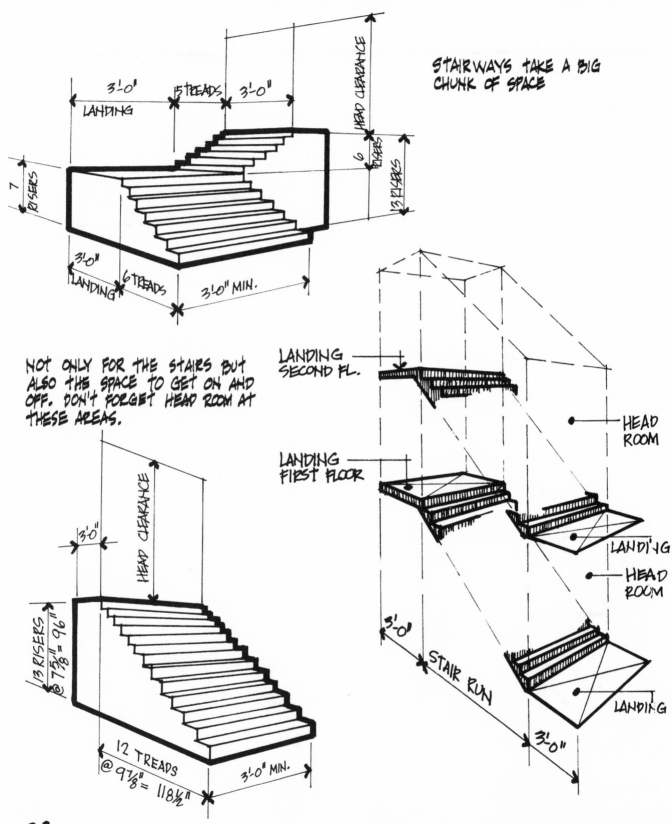

STAIRWAYS TAKE A BIG
CHUNK OF SPACE

3'-0"
LANDING

5 TREADS

3'-0"

HEAD CLEARANCE

6 RISERS

7 RISERS

13 RISERS

3'-0"
LANDING

6 TREADS

3'-0" MIN.

NOT ONLY FOR THE STAIRS BUT
ALSO THE SPACE TO GET ON AND
OFF. DON'T FORGET HEAD ROOM AT
THESE AREAS.

3'-0"

HEAD CLEARANCE

13 RISERS @ 7 3/8" = 96"

12 TREADS
@ 9 7/8" = 118 1/2"

3'-0" MIN.

LANDING
SECOND FL.

LANDING
FIRST FLOOR

HEAD
ROOM

LANDING

HEAD
ROOM

3'-0"

STAIR RUN

3'-0"

LANDING

28

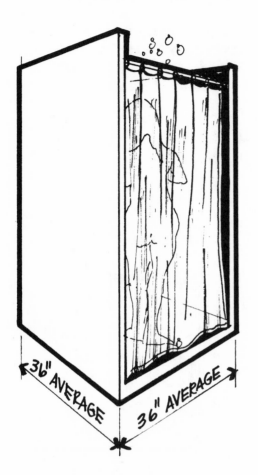

36" AVERAGE

36" AVERAGE

BATHROOMS HAVE SPACES TO CONSIDER — TUB, SINK, SHOWER, JOHN.

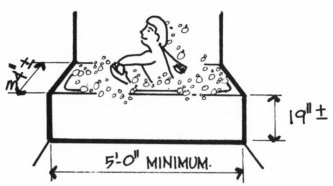

5'-0" MINIMUM.

19" ±

THE FIREPLACE IS ANOTHER BIG CHUNK OF SPACE, AND VERY CENTRAL TO THE THEME OF THE INTERIOR. WHEN YOU SEE A GOOD ONE USE IT IN YOUR DESIGN, BUT BE SURE IT WILL LOOK GOOD IN THE SIZE ROOM YOU PLAN. A BIG FIREPLACE IN A SMALL ROOM IS OVERPOWERING AND A SMALL ONE IN A BIG ROOM IS LOST. REMEMBER THE BRICK WORK RUNS FROM BASEMENT TO ROOF AND THE MORE FLUES IT HAS THE BIGGER THE CHIMNEY. EVEN A WOOD STOVE CHIMNEY WILL TAKE A LOT OF SPACE FROM BASEMENT TO ROOF.

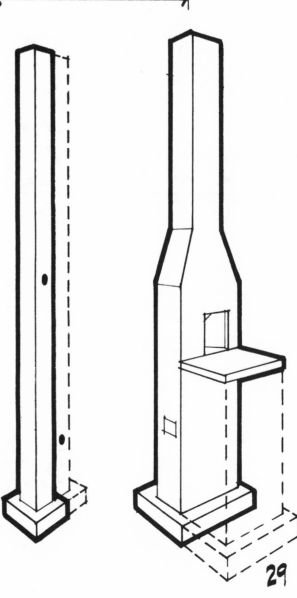

DESIGN

THE KITCHEN HAS THE REFRIGERATOR, RANGE, SINK AND COUNTER SPACE AS MINI-MUM REQUIREMENTS. THEN THERE COULD BE A WALL OVEN, DISH WASHER, BROOM CLOSET AND TABLE OR COUNTER. TAKE NOTES AS YOU SEE LAYOUTS THAT ARE GOOD AND BAD FOR YOU. YOU WONT FORGET IF YOU WRITE IT DOWN.

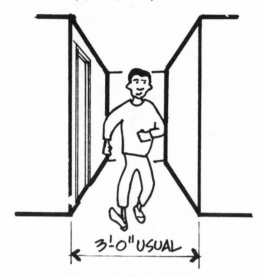

3'-0" USUAL

HALLS TAKE A LOT OF SPACE. THEY SHOULD BE 3'-0" FOR COMFORT, BUT CAN BE NARROWER IF THE LOCAL CODE WILL ALLOW.

A NARROW HALL MAKES FOR A NARROW DOOR AT THE END BECAUSE OF THE FRAMING REQUIRED FOR THE DOOR. MAKING THE TRIM THINNER WILL REQUIRE LESS FRAMING MATERIAL AND THEN A WIDER DOOR.

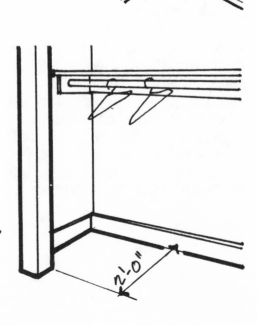

3"

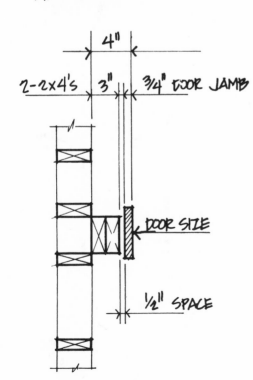

4"

2-2x4's 3" 3/4" DOOR JAMB

DOOR SIZE

1/2" SPACE

A CLOTHING CLOSET SHOULD BE 2'-0" CLEAR FOR HANG-ING GARMENTS....

2'-0"

30

OTHER, AND VERY IMPORTANT, CONSIDERATIONS IN DESIGN ARE: GROUND SLOPE, SUN, AND TREES. WITH THE COST OF FUEL THE ENERGY EFFICIENT HOUSE LOOKS MIGHTY GOOD. WE CAN, AT LEAST, TAKE ADVANTAGE OF SUN, SHADE AND WIND BUFFERS.

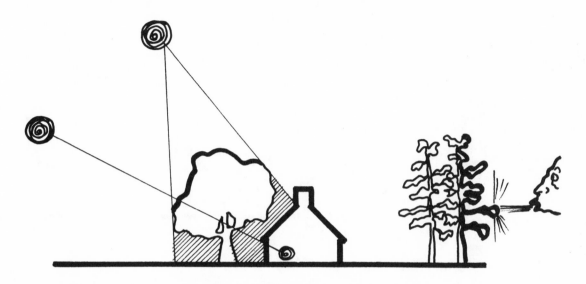

IDEAL CONDITIONS
1. SUMMER SUN SHADED BY LEAFY TREE.
2. WINTER SUN IN HOUSE WHEN LEAVES FALL.
3. NORTH WINTER WINDS BLOCKED BY PINE TREES.

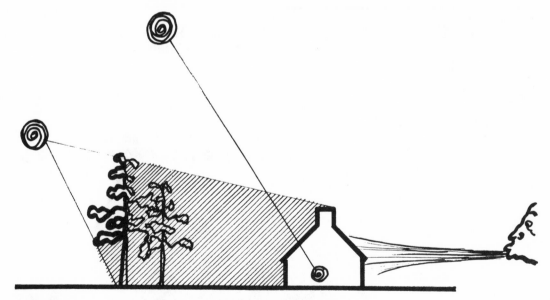

BAD CONDITIONS
1. SUMMER SUN COOKS HOUSE.
2. WINTER SUN BLOCKED BY PINE TREES.
3. NORTH WINTER WINDS CHILL HOUSE.

31

DESIGN

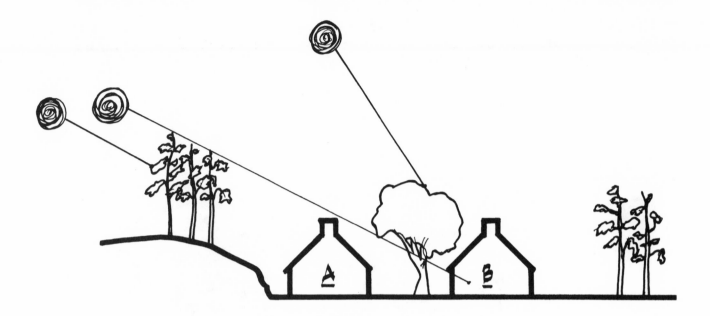

HOUSE "B" LOCATED BETTER THAN HOUSE "A".

HOUSE "A"
1. WINTER SUN BLOCKED BY PINES
2. WATER RUN OFF FROM HILL COULD CAUSE DAMP BASEMENT
3. SUMMER SUN COOKS HOUSE.

HOUSE "B"
1. SUMMER SUN BLOCKED BY LEAFY TREE.
2. WINTER SUN IN HOUSE WHEN LEAVES FALL.
3. NORTH WINTER WINDS BLOCKED BY PINE TREES. BOTH HOUSES BENEFIT BY THIS.

IF THE LAND SLOPES ENOUGH TO THE SOUTH AND THE WINTER SUN IS NOT BLOCKED, THEN AN UNDERGROUND HOUSE SHOULD BE CONSIDERED. TRY TO KEEP SOME LEAFY SHADE TREES TO BLOCK THE SUMMER SUN.

A GOOD QUICK SURVEY METHOD FOR FINDING THE SLOPE OF THE GROUND IS TO USE A SIMPLE CARPENTER'S LEVEL, A FEW WOOD STAKES AND A GOOD EYEBALL.

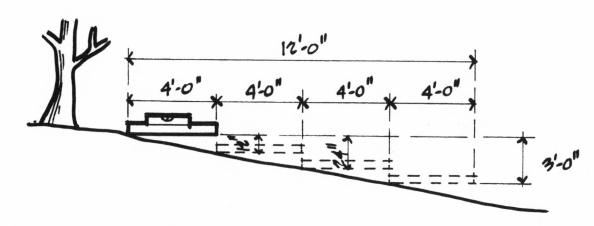

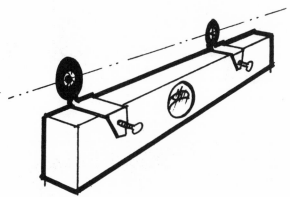

STANLEY TOOLS MAKES AN INEXPENSIVE SET OF LEVEL SIGHTS THAT CLAMP ONTO A WOOD CARPENTERS LEVEL. GOOD ACCURACY CAN BE ACHIEVED WITH EITHER SYSTEM, CERTAINLY GOOD ENOUGH TO DESIGN WITH, IF YOU CAN BORROW A FRIEND'S BUILDERS LEVEL (TRANSIT), SO MUCH THE BETTER, BUT NOT NECESSARY.

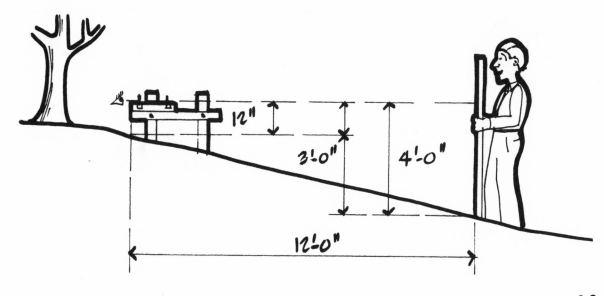

DESIGN

AS FOR STRUCTURAL DESIGN, CHECK THE HOUSES YOU VISIT. GO DOWN TO THE BASE-MENT AND PACE OFF THE SPANS OF THE FLOOR JOISTS AND BEAMS.

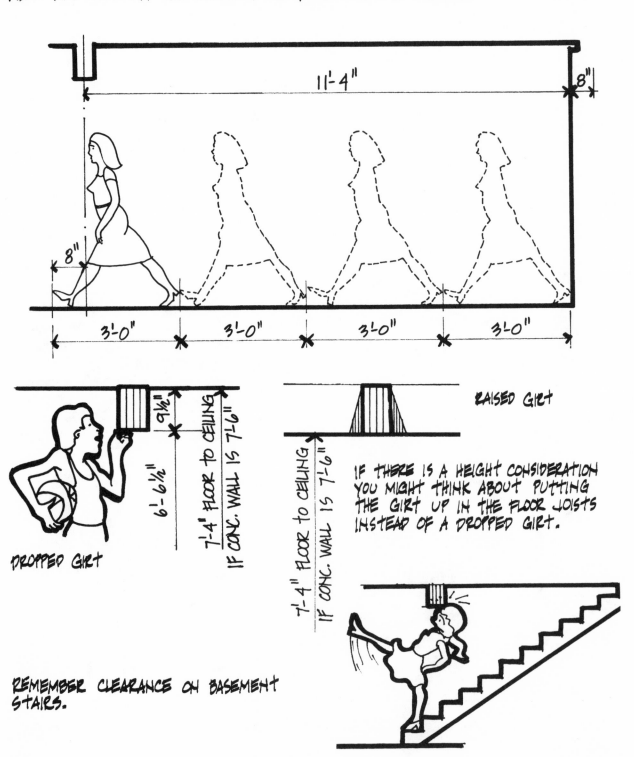

11'-4"

8"

8"

3'-0" 3'-0" 3'-0" 3'-0"

9½"

6'-6½"

7'-4" FLOOR TO CEILING
IF CONC. WALL IS 7'-6"

DROPPED GIRT

RAISED GIRT

7'-4" FLOOR TO CEILING
IF CONC. WALL IS 7'-6"

IF THERE IS A HEIGHT CONSIDERATION YOU MIGHT THINK ABOUT PUTTING THE GIRT UP IN THE FLOOR JOISTS INSTEAD OF A DROPPED GIRT.

REMEMBER CLEARANCE ON BASEMENT STAIRS.

34

COUNT THE JOISTS FOR SPACINGS. LOOK IN THE ATTIC FOR RAFTER SIZES AND SPACING. CHECK A SAGGING ROOF TOO; IT TELLS YOU WHAT NOT TO DO. IF THE DISHES RATTLE WHEN YOU WALK ACROSS THE FLOOR, THAT TELLS YOU SOMETHING TOO. CHECK NEW CONSTRUCTION.

HMMM.....
2x10 JOISTS AT 16" ON CENTER WITH 6 SPACES BETWEEN POSTS MEANS 8'-0" SPAN. BEAMS ARE 4-2x10's AND IT FEELS SOLID UPSTAIRS. I'LL USE THE SAME STUFF IN MY NEW HOUSE.

USE THE CODE BOOKS; THEY WILL TELL YOU THE SIZE AND SPANS FOR THE VARIOUS FRAMING CONDITIONS.

TABLE 1 MAXIMUM SPANS FOR GIRDERS	
SIZE	1 STORY
4x6	6'-0"

TABLE 2 MAXIMUM SPANS FOR FLOOR JOISTS		
SIZE	NO 1.	NO 2.
2x6	9'-1"	8'-6"

DESIGN

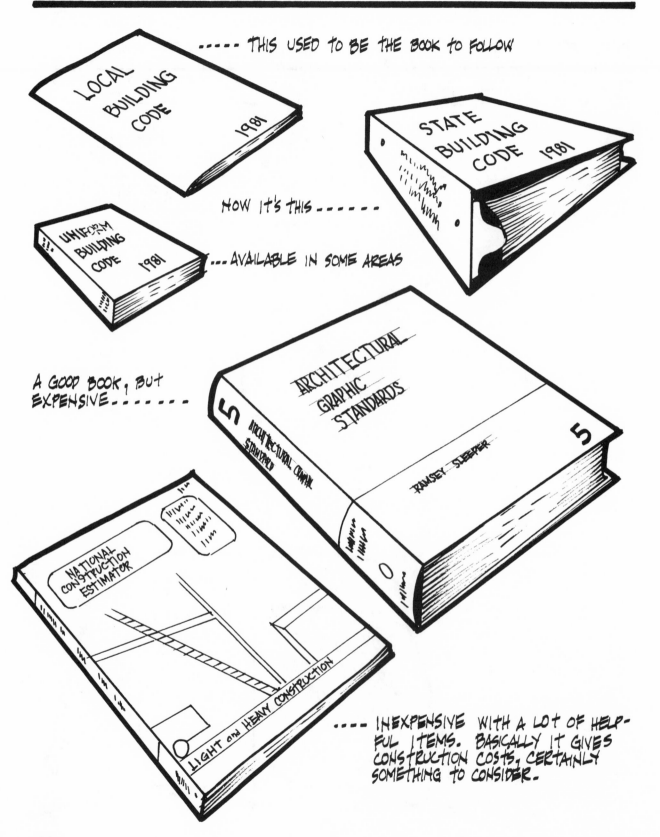

LOCAL BUILDING CODE 1981

----- THIS USED TO BE THE BOOK TO FOLLOW

NOW IT'S THIS ------

STATE BUILDING CODE 1981

UNIFORM BUILDING CODE 1981

...AVAILABLE IN SOME AREAS

A GOOD BOOK, BUT EXPENSIVE--------

ARCHITECTURAL GRAPHIC STANDARDS

RAMSEY SLEEPER

5

NATIONAL CONSTRUCTION ESTIMATOR

LIGHT and HEAVY CONSTRUCTION

---- INEXPENSIVE WITH A LOT OF HELP-FUL ITEMS. BASICALLY IT GIVES CONSTRUCTION COSTS, CERTAINLY SOMETHING TO CONSIDER.

ANY LARGE DEPARTMENT STORE CATALOG HAS A WEALTH OF INFORMATION. ANY ITEM IN HOUSE, GARAGE, GARDEN OR SHOP IS COVERED BY SIZE, SHAPE, COLOR AND WEIGHT.

LOCAL LUMBER YARDS SOMETIMES HAVE FREE OR INEXPENSIVE DESIGN CATALOGS.

WILL A 4x10 BEAM WORK HERE?

CHECK WITH THE BUILDING INSPECTOR; HE IS THERE TO HELP YOU. DON'T TRY TO SLIP ANYTHING BY HIM—HE OR SHE HAS WAYS OF MAKING UP FOR IT TEN TIMES OVER. ONE OTHER CAUTION: CHECK WITH BUILDERS OR CARPENTERS ABOUT THE IN-SPECTORS ABILITY TO DEAL WITH THE OP-POSITE SEX BE IT MALE OR FEMALE. I HAVE RUN ACROSS SOME MALE INSPECTORS THAT GIVE WOMEN A HARD TIME. DON'T FIGHT HIM, TRY USING A MALE FRIEND TO DEAL THROUGH. OF COURSE FOLLOW THE CODES.

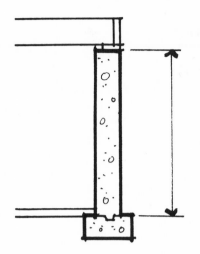

FOUNDATION WALL HEIGHTS ARE PRETTY MUCH CONTROLLED BY THE LOCAL CONCRETE CONTRACTOR. HIS FORMS ARE JUST SO HIGH, LIMITING THE HEIGHT OF THE CONCRETE POUR. IN MY AREA, 7'-6" IS THE COMMON POUR, BUT ANY HEIGHT CAN BE POURED IF THE FORMS ARE MODIFIED. IT ALWAYS COSTS MORE IF YOU STRAY FROM THE NORMAL CONDITIONS.

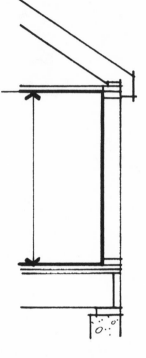

FIRST AND SECOND FLOOR MINIMUM CEILING HEIGHTS ARE SOMETIMES SET BY CODE, AND IF NOT, USE YOUR OWN FEELINGS. TRY TO KEEP STUD LENGTHS UNDER 8' FOR ECONOMY.

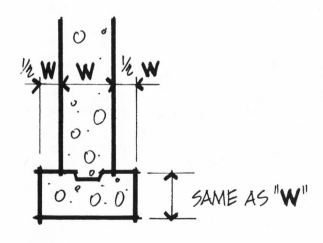

½ W | W | ½ W

SAME AS "W"

CONCRETE WALL THICKNESS IS GENERALLY SET BY CODE, AND THE FOOTINGS ARE TAKEN OFF THAT DIMENSION.

THE BALLOON FRAME IS IDEAL FOR THE ENERGY EFFICIENT HOUSE AND WORTH CONSIDERING WHEN DESIGNING. PUT 2x2 HORIZONTAL NAILERS ON THE STUDS AND YOU HAVE THE "SCANDINAVIAN WALL". IF YOU INSULATE BETWEEN THE STUDS, PUT A VAPOR BARRIER ON THE INSIDE FACE AND THEN THE 2x2's, YOU WILL HAVE AN UNBROK-EN VAPOR BARRIER. A VERY IMPORTANT FACTOR IN INSULATING.

RAFTERS

(NOT PART OF BALLOON FRAME)
2x2 @ 24" O.C.

2x6 STUDS @ 24" O.C. OR 16" O.C.

JOISTS

RIBBON

DROPPED BEAM

JOIST

2x10 SILL

CONC. FOUNDATION

RIGID FOAM

BALLOON FRAME

2x4 STUDS @ 16" O.C.

HEADER

JOISTS

THE STANDARD PLAT-FORM FRAME LEAVES MUCH TO BE DESIRED WHEN IT COMES TO INSULATING, BUT IT IS EASY TO FRAME UP.

RAISED BEAM

HEADER

JOIST

CONC. FOUNDATION

WESTERN OR PLATFORM FRAME

DESIGN

ONCE THE BASIC HOUSE IS DECIDED ON MENTALLY, IT IS TIME TO SKETCH. USE A FELT TIP PEN ON YELLOW SKETCH PAPER (OR ANY CHEAP PAPER). YOU MIGHT WANT TO PUT A PIECE OF GRAPH PAPER UNDER TO HELP WITH THE HORIZONTAL AND VERTICAL LINE WORK. JUST LET YOUR INNER WISDOM GO TO TOWN AND CHECK YOUR NOTES. USE FLAT PAPER FURNITURE CUT OUTS, THE SAME SCALE AS THE FLOOR PLANS FOR ROOM DESIGNING.

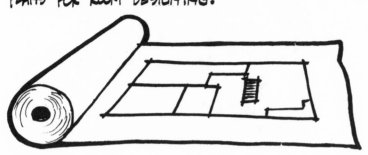

KEEP AN EMPTY WASTE BASKET WITHIN "SHOOTING" RANGE.

WHEN YOU MAKE A GOOD SKETCH, BUT IT NEEDS A CHANGE, JUST LAY THE YELLOW TRACE OVER AND MAKE A NEW SKETCH WITH THE CHANGE. IT IS A FAST WAY TO WORK AND YOU WILL FIND YOUR MIND WORKING FAST TOO.

THIS IS DONE WITH THE EXTERIOR AND INTERIOR DESIGN.

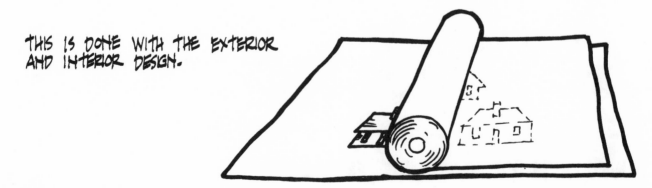

TO FIRM IT UP, DRAW IT FREE HAND ON GRAPH PAPER. THIS WILL GIVE YOU AN IDEA OF SIZES.

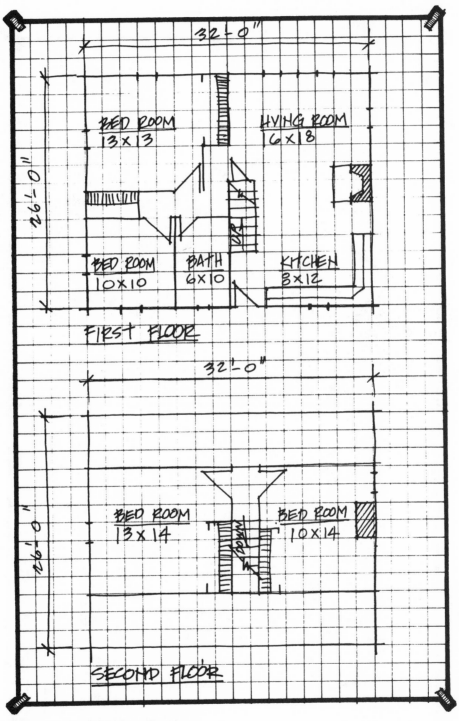

32'-0"

26'-0"

BED ROOM
13 x 13

LIVING ROOM
16 x 18

BED ROOM
10 x 10

BATH
6 x 10

KITCHEN
8 x 12

FIRST FLOOR

32'-0"

26'-0"

BED ROOM
13 x 14

BED ROOM
10 x 14

SECOND FLOOR

ONE SQUARE = 2 FEET

41

DESIGN

DO THE SAME WITH THE EXTERIOR.

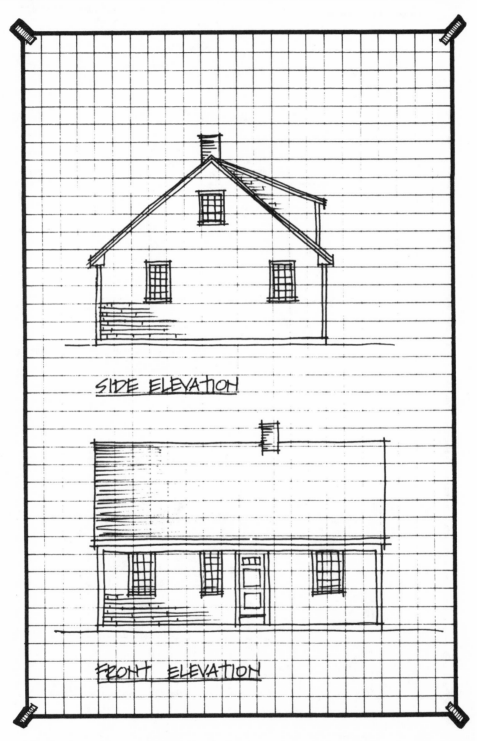

SIDE ELEVATION

FRONT ELEVATION

ONE SQUARE = 2 FEET

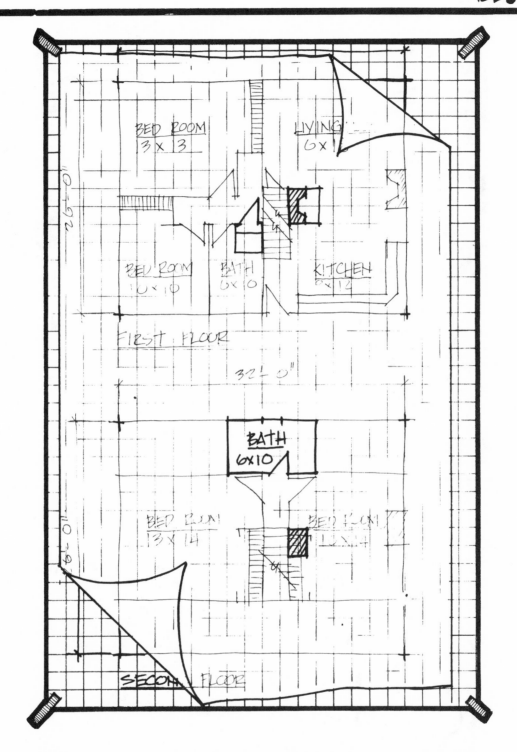

BED ROOM
13 x 13

LIVING
6 x

BED ROOM
6 x 10

BATH
6 x 10

KITCHEN
6 x 12

FIRST FLOOR

32'-0"

BATH
6 x 10

BED ROOM
13 x 14

BED ROOM
13 x 14

SECOND FLOOR

YOU MIGHT WANT TO MAKE MORE CHANGES, USE THE YELLOW TRACING PAPER. YOU CAN
GO FROM THE YELLOW TRACING OR BACK TO THE GRAPH PAPER TO START THE WORKING
DRAWINGS. REMEMBER WHEN USING LINE SKETCHES THE WALL THICKNESS IS NOT
SHOWN; KEEP THAT IN MIND WHEN DIMENSIONING.

PLUMBING VENTS LOOK BAD ON THE ENTRANCE SIDE OF THE ROOF.

YOU NEVER KNOW WHEN YOUR TAPE MEASURE WILL COME IN HANDY.

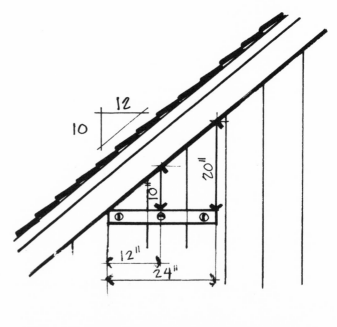

THINK OF THE FUTURE.

USE A CARPENTER'S LEVEL AND A TAPE MEASURE TO FIND THE ROOF PITCH.

3-DRAFTING

YOU DON'T HAVE TO BE A TERRIFIC ARTIST TO BE A GOOD DRAFTSMAN. WHAT IT DOES TAKE IS OBSERVATION AND PRACTICE. TRY TO LEARN WHAT MAKES FOR A GOOD-LOOKING JOB AND THEN PRACTICE THE TECHNIQUES REQUIRED. THE PLANS DON'T HAVE TO BE A FANTASTIC WORK; AS LONG AS THE BUILDER KNOWS WHATS GOING ON THEY WILL BE FINE. WHAT CAN BE DIFFICULT ABOUT RUNNING A PENCIL ALONG A STRAIGHT EDGE OR MEASURING WITH A SCALE? WITH THE INEXPENSIVE CALCULATORS, MATHAMATICS BECOMES FUN (ALMOST). THE ONLY DIFFICULT THING IS THE LETTERING AND IT IS ONLY DIFFICULT (AT FIRST) TO MAKE IT STYLISH, BUT NOT DIFFICULT TO MAKE IT LEGIBLE.

DRAFTING

THE FIRST THINGS TO DECIDE ARE WHAT TO DRAW ON AND WHAT SIZE THE SHEETS WILL BE. BECAUSE FLOOR PLANS ARE TRACED ONE FROM THE OTHER, TRACING PAPER WOULD BE A GOOD CHOICE. THE SHEET SIZE IS DETERMINED BY THE BUILDING SIZE AND THE PRINTING PROCESS. A 2" SPACE ON EACH SIDE AND TOP WITH 3" ON THE BOTTOM ADDED TO THE LENGTH AND WIDTH OF THE HOUSE WILL GIVE THE SIZE SHEET TO USE. THE 2" AND 3" DIMENSIONS ALLOW SPACE FOR DIMENSIONS AND TITLES. A HOUSE 26'x 32', DRAWN AT 1/4" SCALE, WILL USE A SHEET 11 1/2"X 12". IF THE PRINTS ARE TO BE XEROX, THEN THE MAXIMUM SIZE SHEET WILL BE 11"x 17" (CHECK WITH YOUR LOCAL PRINTER). THE 1/2" LOST ON HEIGHT CAN BE FUDGED WITH THE 3" BOTTOM. THE EXTRA 5" CAN BE USED FOR DETAILS. TRY TO KEEP THE DETAILS THAT ARE RELATIVE TO THE PLAN ON THE SAME SHEET. IF THE PRINTS ARE TO BE THE OZALID PROCESS, THEN A MUCH LARGER SHEET CAN BE USED, BUT THE 2" AND 3" DIMENSIONS SHOULD BE USED IN FIGURING THE SHEET SIZE.

THE NUMBER OF SHEETS IS DETERMINED BY THE SHEET SIZE, AND BUILDING INSPECTOR'S REQUIREMENTS. A LARGE SHEET COULD HAVE ALL THE PLANS ON ONE, A SMALL SHEET REQUIRES MANY SHEETS.

A GOOD SET OF WORKING DRAWINGS WOULD BE:

FOUNDATION PLAN	1/4"=1'-0"
FLOOR PLANS	1/4"=1'-0"
ELEVATIONS	1/4"=1'-0" OR 1/8"=1'-0"
SECTION THROUGH BUILDING	3/8"=1'-0" (SHOWS CONSTRUCTION)
DETAILS	1 1/2"=1'-0" (BETTER UNDERSTANDING OF CONSTRUCTION)
CABINET ELEVATIONS	1/4"=1'-0"
FIREPLACE ELEVATION	1/16"=1'-0"
FLOOR FRAMING	1/16"=1'-0" OR 1/4"=1'-0"
ELECTRICAL PLAN	1/4"=1'-0" (CAN BE ON FLOOR PLAN)
PLOT PLAN	1"=20'

THE FIRST FOUR WOULD BE THE MINIMUM REQUIREMENTS.
ELEVATIONS CAN BE AT 1/8" SCALE TO CUT DOWN ON THE NUMBER OF SHEETS.

WHEN THE NUMBER OF SHEETS IS DECIDED, CUT THEM ALL AT THE SAME TIME OR USE PRECUT SHEETS.

DETERMINE SHEET SIZE AND CUT AS MANY AS NEEDED.

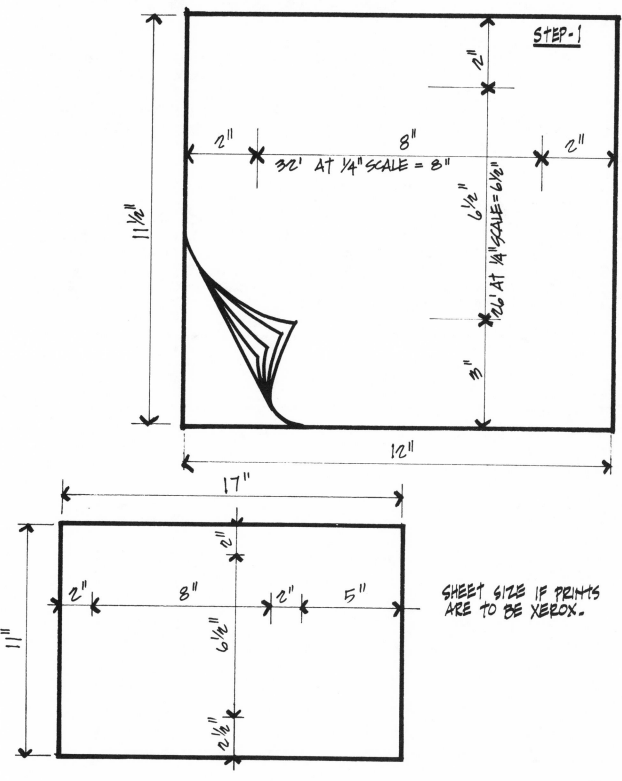

STEP-1

2"

2"   8"   2"
32' AT ¼" SCALE = 8"

11½"

6½"
26' AT ¼" SCALE = 6½"

3"

12"

17"

2"

2"   8"   2"   5"

11"

6½"

2½"

SHEET SIZE IF PRINTS
ARE TO BE XEROX.

DRAFTING

TAPE THE FIRST SHEET DOWN AND YOU ARE READY TO LAY OUT THE FIRST FLOOR PLAN.
USE A 2H LEAD WITH A LIGHT TOUCH, JUST DARK ENOUGH TO SEE WITHOUT TOO MUCH
TROUBLE.

ALWAYS TWIRL THE PENCIL WITH THE FINGERS WHEN
DRAWING HORIZONTAL AND VERTICAL LINES. THIS WILL
KEEP THE WEAR EVEN ON THE POINT AND THE LINE
WILL BE A CONSISTENT THICKNESS. IT TAKES A
LITTLE GETTING USED TO, BUT IS A MUST.

START WITH THE PERIMETER OF THE HOUSE AND THEN THE
PARTITIONS; DON'T WORRY ABOUT DOORS AND WINDOWS YET.
DRAW THE EXTERIOR WALLS 5" (AT 1/4" SCALE CLOSE IS
GOOD ENOUGH) IF STUDS ARE TO BE 2x4 AND 7" IF 2x6. THE INTERIOR PARTITIONS
WILL BE 2x4 SO 4½ FOR THEM. THESE DIMENSIONS TAKE INTO ACCOUNT THE WALL
MATERIAL, STUD, SIDING, SHEATHING, SHEETROCK.

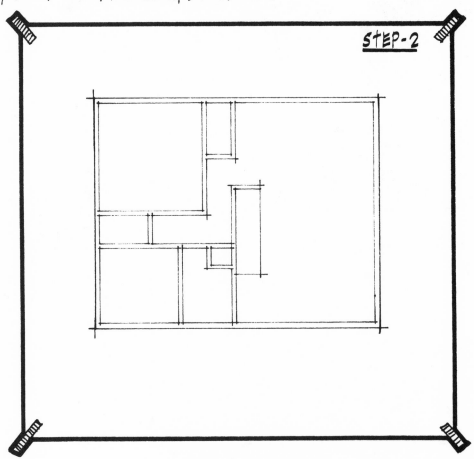

STEP-2

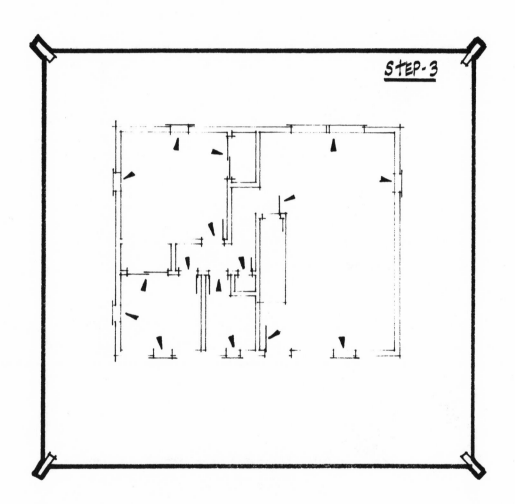

STEP-3

LOCATE DOORS AND WINDOWS.

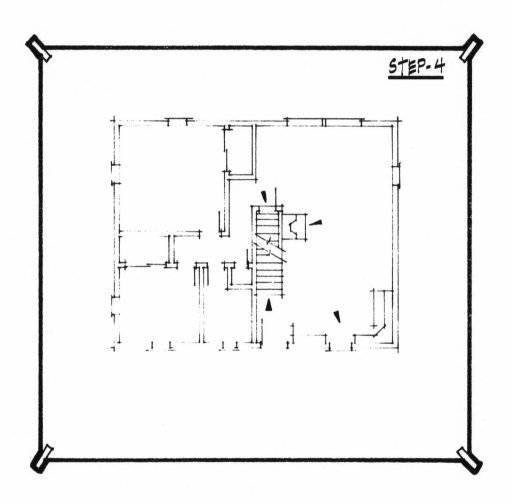

STEP-4

LOCATE STAIRS, FIREPLACE AND KITCHEN CABINETS.

LOCATE BATHROOM FIXTURES, KITCHEN SINK, RANGE AND REFRIGERATOR. WHEN SATISFIED THAT ALL IS WELL, DARKEN THE LINE WORK TO MAKE THINGS CLEARER. SAVE THE FINAL PUNCHING UP (DARK AND HEAVY) UNTIL AFTER THE DIMENSIONS ARE ON. IF LINE WORK IS HEAVIED UP AND WORK CONTINUES, THE SHEET WILL GET DIRTY.

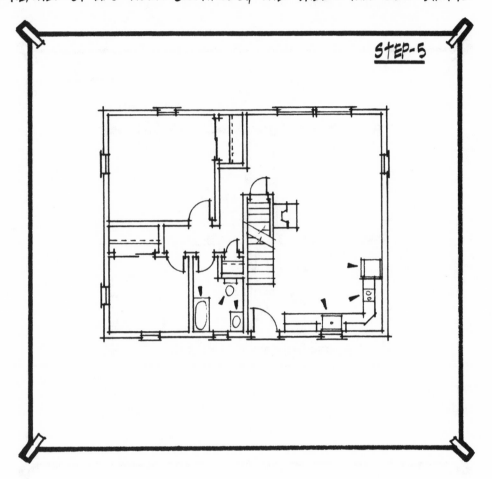

STEP-5

WHERE LINES CROSS AT CORNERS, EXTEND THEM PAST EACH OTHER.

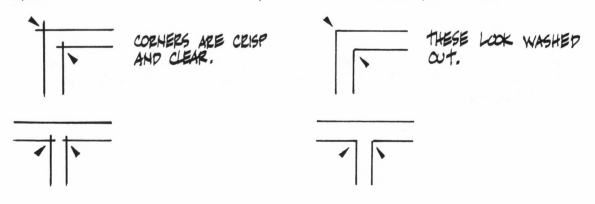

CORNERS ARE CRISP AND CLEAR.

THESE LOOK WASHED OUT.

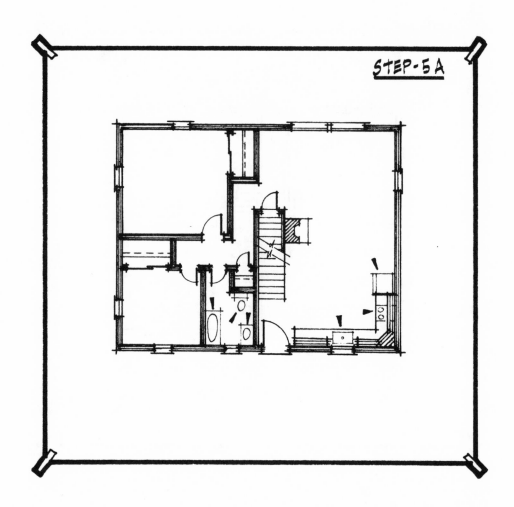

STEP-5A

FILLING IN THE PARTITIONS WITH LIGHTER PARALLEL LINES HELPS to SHOW THEM UP, HOWEVER DIMENSION LINES ARE NOT QUITE AS CLEAR. IT IS NOT NECESSARY to DO, IT JUST DRESSES THE DRAWING UP.

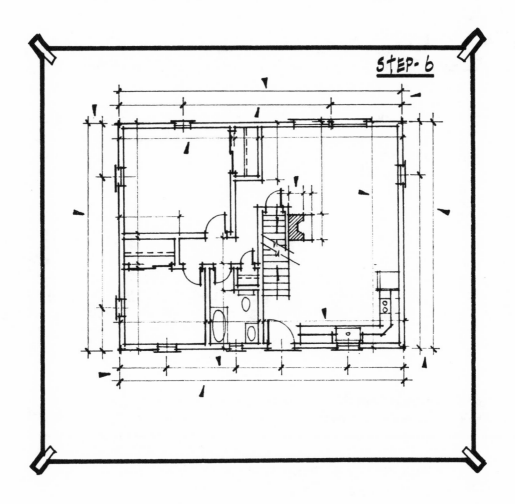

STEP-6

DIMENSION LINES COME NEXT AND THEY SHOULD BE LIGHTER THAN THE PARTITION LINES, BUT DARK ENOUGH TO BE POSITIVE. THE WALLS WANT TO JUMP OUT AT YOU.

53

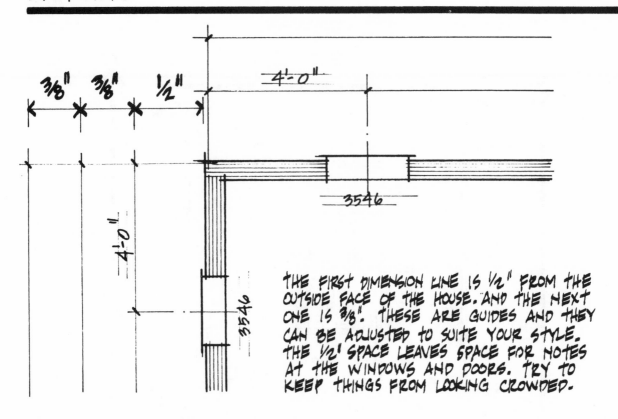

3/8"   3/8"   1/2"

4'-0"

4'-0"

3546

3546

THE FIRST DIMENSION LINE IS 1/2" FROM THE OUTSIDE FACE OF THE HOUSE. AND THE NEXT ONE IS 3/8". THESE ARE GUIDES AND THEY CAN BE ADJUSTED TO SUITE YOUR STYLE. THE 1/2' SPACE LEAVES SPACE FOR NOTES AT THE WINDOWS AND DOORS. TRY TO KEEP THINGS FROM LOOKING CROWDED.

THERE ARE THREE BASIC SYMBOLS FOR TERMINATING DIMENSION LINES:

I FAVOR THIS SIMPLE 45° FREE HAND SLASH: IT'S EASY AND CLEAR.....

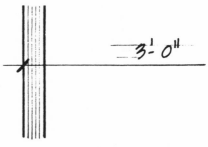

3'-0"

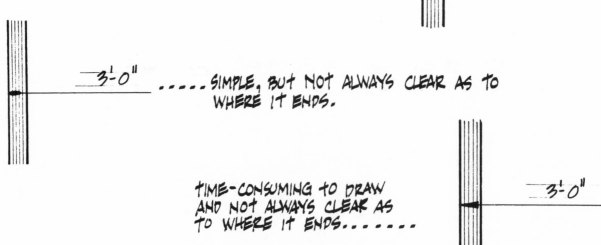

3'-0" ..... SIMPLE, BUT NOT ALWAYS CLEAR AS TO WHERE IT ENDS.

TIME-CONSUMING TO DRAW AND NOT ALWAYS CLEAR AS TO WHERE IT ENDS........

3'-0"

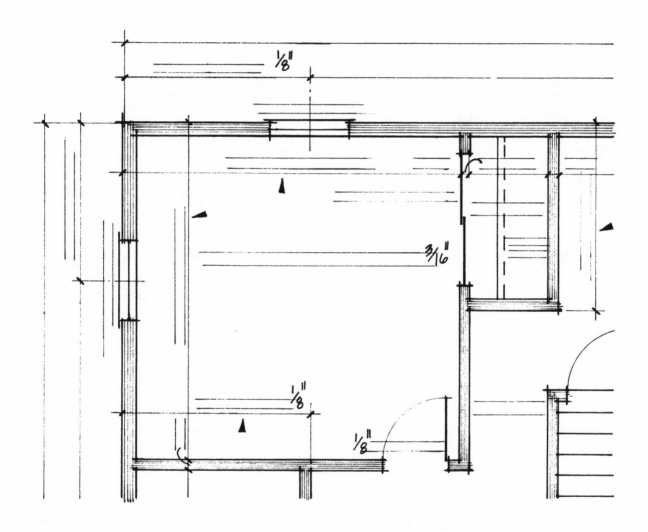

INSIDE DIMENSION LINES ARE KEPT TOWARD THE WALLS TO ALLOW FOR ROOM LABELING AND UNINTERRUPTED DIMENSION NUMBERS. THE DIMENSION SHOULD BE AT THE MID POINT OF WHAT IT IS DESCRIBING. CLARITY IS IMPAIRED IF A DIMENSION RUNS THROUGH IT. SOMETIMES IT CAN'T BE HELPED. DOORS AND WINDOWS ARE LOCATED ON THEIR CENTER LINE.

THERE IS A CHOICE TO BE MADE WHEN DIMENSIONING INSIDE PARTITIONS AND EACH HAS ITS GOOD AND BAD POINTS.

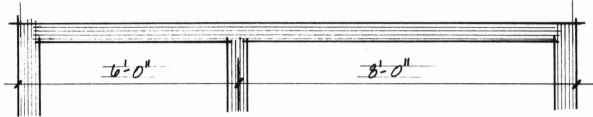

USING THE CENTER LINE OF PARTITIONS IS GOOD, BUT MAKE SURE TO BE CONSISTENT. THE CARPENTER THEN KNOWS THAT HE MUST LOCATE EACH PARTITION FACE OFF THE CENTER LINE ON THE PLANS.

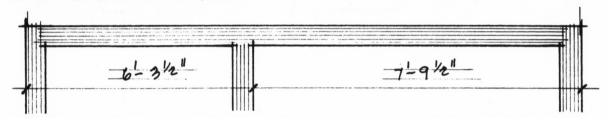

DIMENSION LINES TO ONE FACE OF A PARTITION (EXCLUDING THE EXTERIOR WHICH IS ALWAYS TO THE OUTSIDE FACE OF STUD) CAN BE CONFUSING. MANY MISTAKES ARE MADE BY PUTTING THE PARTITION ON THE WRONG SIDE OF THE LINE.

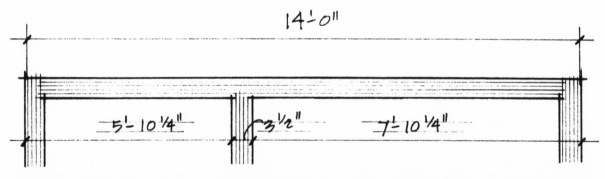

TO DIMENSION BOTH SIDES OF THE PARTITION IS A LOT MORE WORK FOR THE DRAFTS-MAN, BUT VERY NICE FOR THE CARPENTER. MOST INTERIOR PARTITIONS ARE 3½" STUDS WHICH WILL CAUSE QUITE A FEW FRACTIONS TO COME UP IN THE DIMEN-SIONS; THAT IS WHY SOME DRAFTSMEN USE 4" FOR THIS DIMENSION. THE CARPEN-TER LAYS OUT THE ROOMS, USING THE 4" AND THEN ADJUSTS FOR THE ACTUAL 3½" WALL.

WHATEVER SYSTEM IS USED, THE SUM OF THE INSIDE DIMENSIONS MUST EQUAL THE EXTERIOR DIMENSION; ALWAYS CHECK THIS OUT. NEVER USE A DIMENSION LESS THAN ⅛" ANYWHERE, IT'S A HOUSE NOT A PIANO. STAY WITH ¼" MIN. FOR DIMENSIONS.

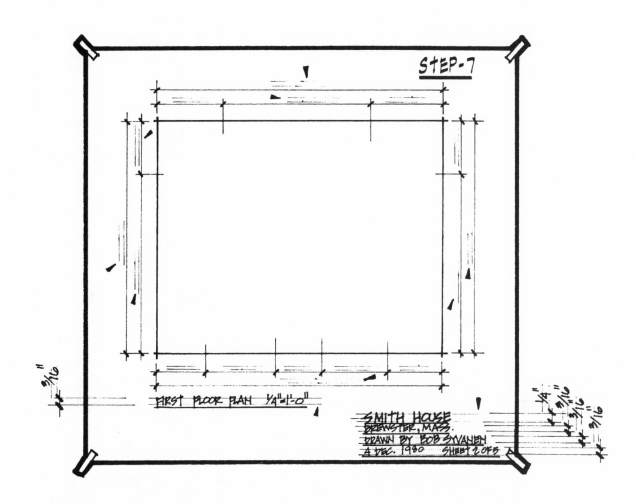

STEP-7

FIRST FLOOR PLAN 1/4"=1'-0"

SMITH HOUSE
BREWSTER, MASS.
DRAWN BY BOB SYVANEN
4 DEC. 1980   SHEET 2 OF 3

PUT IN ALL THE LETTERING GUIDE LINES AND DON'T BE AFRAID IF THEY SHOW UP ON THE PRINTS, I THINK THEY ADD TO THE LOOKS OF THE DRAWING. THE SIZES I USE MIGHT NOT SUIT YOU; USE THEM AS A GUIDE. PUT THE DIMENSIONS IN AFTER ALL THE GUIDE LINES ARE IN. DON'T WORRY IF THE PLAN DOES NOT MEASURE WHAT THE DIMENSION READS UNLESS IT IS VERY MUCH OUT OF SCALE. IT'S GOOD IF IT IS DIMENSIONED AS YOU WANT AND THE TOTALS ADD UP. I LIKE TO SAVE ALL THE LARGE LETTERING FOR LAST, AND DO ALL THE SHEETS AT THE SAME TIME, THE SHEETS STAY CLEANER AND THE LETTERING IS MORE CONSISTENT.

DRAFTING

VERTICAL LETTERING IS PRINT-
ED AS IF THE SHEET IS IN
THIS POSITION ----------

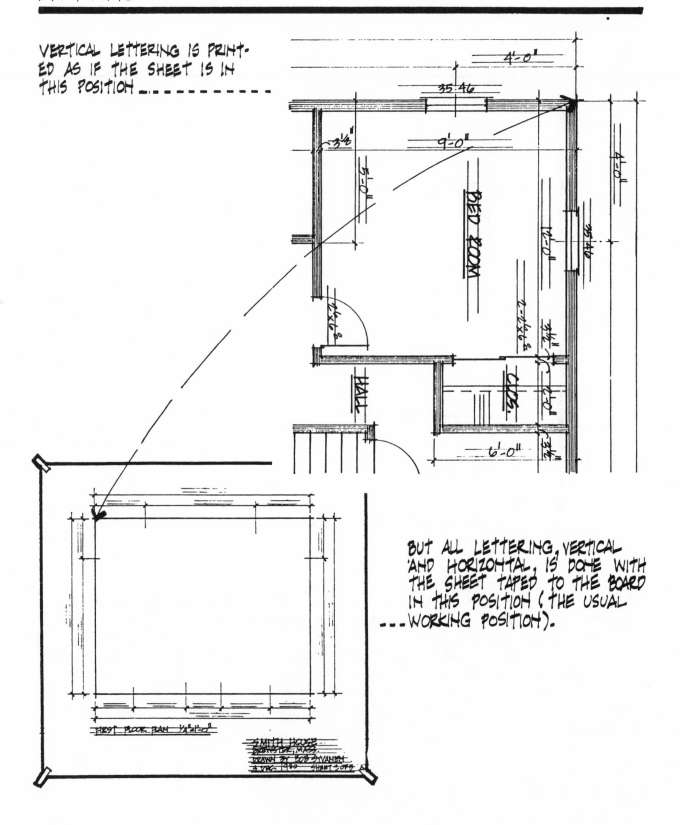

BED ROOM

HALL

FIRST FLOOR PLAN 1/4"=1'-0"

SMITH HOUSE
BREWSTER, MASS.
DRAWN BY BOB SIVANEN
4 DEC. 1980   SHEET 2 OF 5

BUT ALL LETTERING, VERTICAL
'AND HORIZONTAL, IS DONE WITH
THE SHEET TAPED TO THE BOARD
IN THIS POSITION (THE USUAL
--- WORKING POSITION).

THE FOUNDATION PLAN IS TRACED FROM THE FIRST FLOOR PLAN.

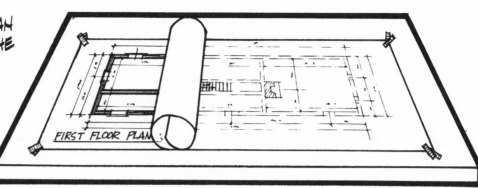

FIRST FLOOR PLAN

STEP· 8

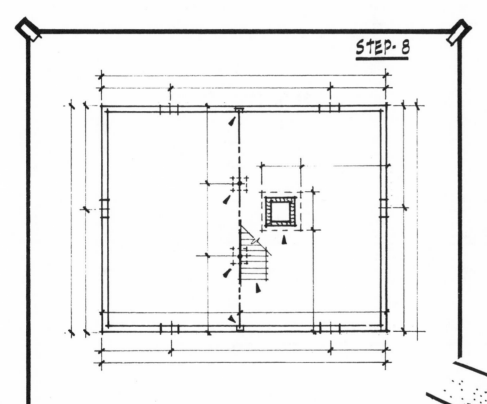

LOCATE CHIMNEY FOOTINGS, COLUMNS, BEAM POCKETS, WINDOWS, SEPTIC LINE, WATER LINE AND ANY SLEEVES GOING THROUGH THE FOUNDATION WALL. THE DRAWING STEPS ARE THE SAME AS THE FIRST FLOOR PLAN.

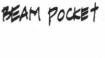

BEAM POCKET

IF THE PRINTS ARE TO BE OF THE OZALID PROCESS, COLOR THE CONCRETE WALLS, WITH A BLUE PENCIL, ON THE BACK FACE OF THE DRAWINGS. MAKE IT MEDIUM DARK AND IT WILL SHOW A NICE SHADING ON THE PRINTS. DON'T COLOR THE WINDOW OPENINGS.

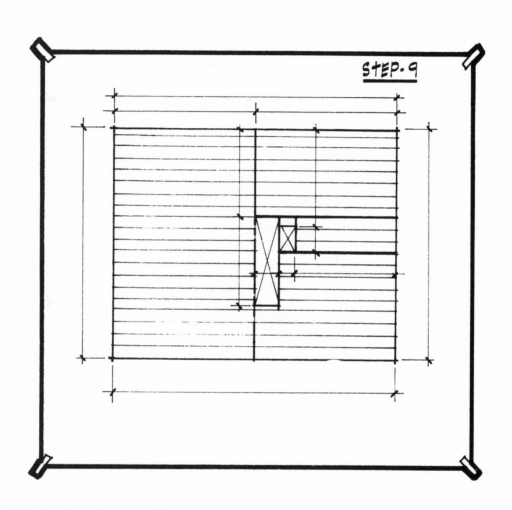

LAY ANOTHER SHEET OVER THE FOUNDATION PLAN AND LAY OUT THE FLOOR FRAMING PLAN. IT IS A GOOD SAFE WAY TO DRAW THE FRAMING BECAUSE THE STAIRS, CHIMNEY AND FLOOR BEAM ARE RIGHT THERE TO SEE. A SIMPLE WAY TO DRAW THE JOISTS IS TO TAKE THE LENGTH X 12" TO GET THE TOTAL INCHES. THEN DIVIDE BY 16" TO GET THE NUMBER OF JOIST SPACES. THE CALCULATOR DOES A GREAT JOB HERE. FIND A SCALE THAT IS CLOSE ENOUGH TO ANGLE FROM ONE SIDE TO THE OTHER (SEE ILLUSTRATIONS FOR SIDING SPACING ON PAGE 62) AND MARK THE SPACES. USE SINGLE LINES FOR ALL MEMBERS, JOISTS, HEADERS, BRIDGING, BLOCKING.

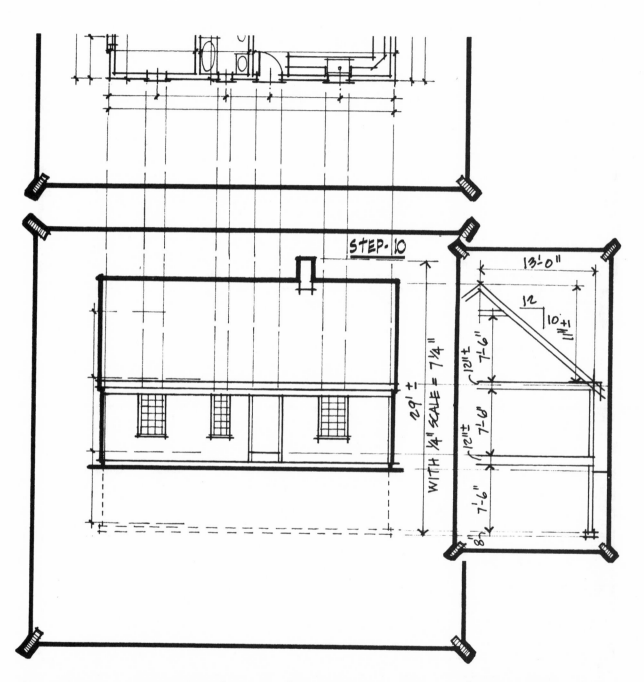

STEP·10

WITH ¼" SCALE = 7¼"

29'±

13'-0"

12

10'±

7'-6"

12"±

7'-6"

12"±

7'-6"

8'-6"

THE ELEVATIONS ARE PROJECTED OFF THE FLOOR PLAN AND A ¼" SCALE SECTION. IF THE ELEVATIONS ARE DRAWN AT ⅛" SCALE, EVERYTHING MUST BE SCALED.

TEXTURES ARE DRAWN TO SUIT YOUR ARTISTIC SENSE. THEY SHOULD RESEMBLE THE MATERIAL USED.

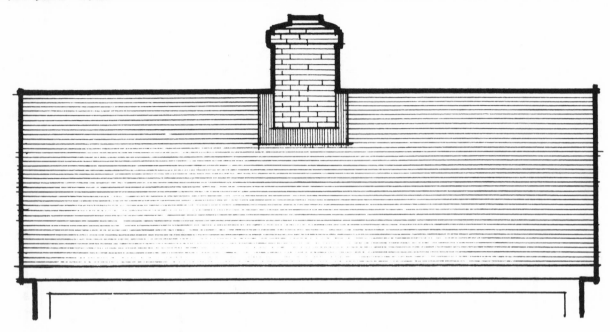

ROOF WITH CLOSE PARALLEL LINES SIMULATE SHINGLE COURSES.

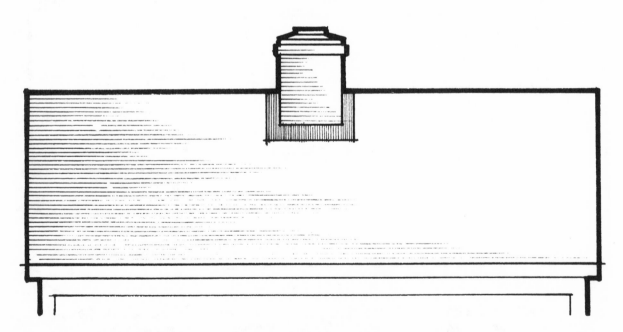

ROOF TEXTURE BROKEN BACK TO SIMULATE SUN ON ROOF.
THE SAME FOR BRICK WORK.

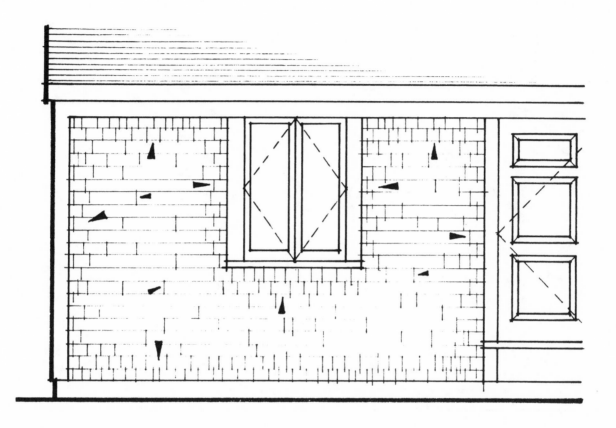

SHINGLES CAN BE PLAIN HORIZONTAL LINES, BROKEN BACK LIKE THE ROOF, OR USE
CONTINUOUS WITH VERTICAL SHINGLE LINES. ACCENT THE CORNERS, WINDOWS, DOORS,
EAVES, AND THE BOTTOM COURSE OF SHINGLES. BY USING MORE VERTICAL LINES AT THESE
AREAS. USE A TRIANGLE AGAINST A PARALLEL STRAIGHT EDGE TO DO THIS. SPOT A FEW
VERTICAL LINES IN THE EMPTY SPACES.

DRAW THE ROOF PITCH WITH THE ADJUSTABLE TRIANGLE. LAY OUT, ON PAPER, A HORIZONTAL 12" LINE AND A VERTICAL 10" LINE AND CONNECT. THESE POINTS TO GET THE PITCH ANGLE. SET TRIANGLE TO THIS.

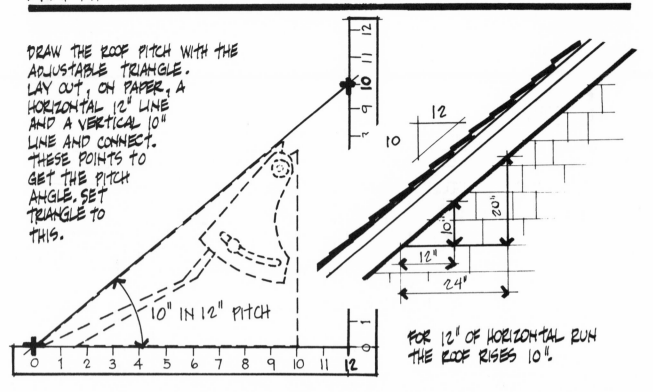

10" IN 12" PITCH

FOR 12" OF HORIZONTAL RUN THE ROOF RISES 10".

SIDING IS DRAWN USING THE DIMENSION OF THE MATERIAL, 5" SHINGLE COURSES, 4", 5", OR 10" CLAP BOARDS AND 4" TO 10" VERTICAL AND DIAGONAL SIDING.

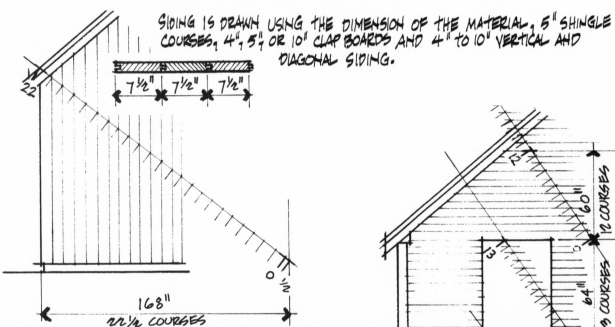

7½"   7½"   7½"

168"
22½ COURSES

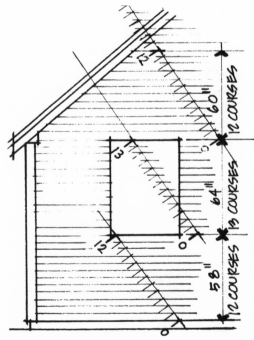

PUT THE SHINGLE COURSES ON AS THEY WOULD BE DONE BY THE CARPENTER. ANGLE THE SCALE TO GET THE RIGHT NUMBER OF COURSES FOR VERTICAL AND HORIZONTAL SIDING.

64

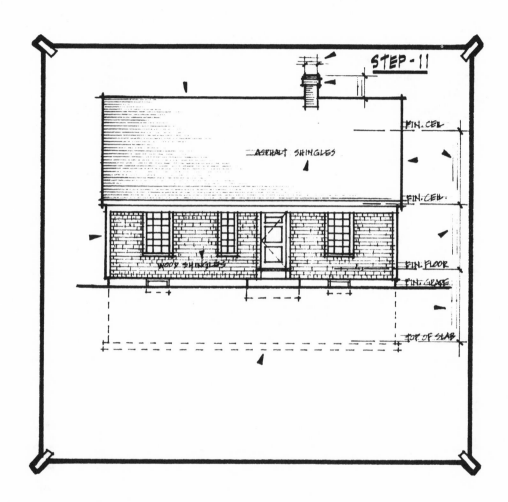

STEP-11

ASPHALT SHINGLES

FIN. CEIL.

FIN. CEIL.

WOOD SHINGLES

FIN. FLOOR

FIN. GRADE

TOP OF SLAB

THIS IS A GOOD PLACE TO SHOW THE RELATIONSHIP BETWEEN THE FOUNDATION AND THE FINISH-
ED GRADE. DIMENSION THE FLOOR HEIGHTS AND CHIMNEY SIZE. HEAVY UP THE WHOLE DRAW-
ING AND IN PARTICULAR, THE FINISH GRADE AND THE OUTLINE OF THE HOUSE.
THE MAIN STEPS, 1 THROUGH 11, ARE FOLLOWED BY THE DETAILS. THERE SHOULD BE AT
LEAST ON SECTION THROUGH THE BUILDING SHOWING FOUNDATION, EXTERIOR WALL,
AND ROOF.

DRAFTING

DETAILS CAN BE DRAWN AT ANY TIME. MAKE SKETCHES OF THEM AS YOU GO ALONG. THESE DETAILS WILL MAKE THINGS EASIER FOR THE BUILDER AND SHOW THE BUILDING INSPECTOR HOW THE HOUSE IS TO BE BUILT. HE CAN TELL YOU BEFORE IT'S BUILT IF IT IS ACCEPTABLE.

WHEN DRAWING DETAILS, PUNCH UP THE SECTIONS THAT THE DRAWING CUTS THROUGH. THINGS LIKE 2X4 PLATES, JOISTS, TRIM AND FOUNDATION.

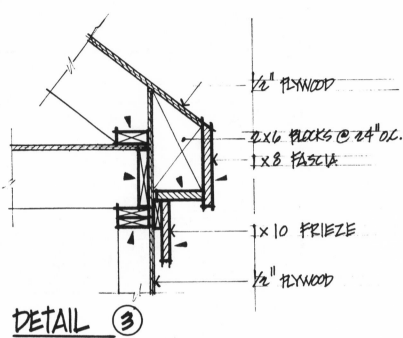

½" PLYWOOD

2X6 BLOCKS @ 24" O.C.

1X8 FASCIA

1X10 FRIEZE

½" PLYWOOD

DETAIL ③

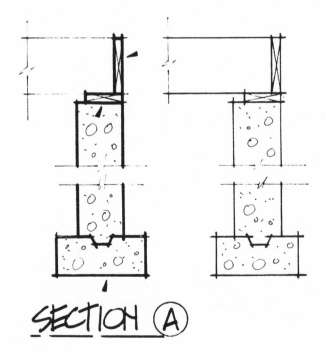

SECTION Ⓐ

DRAW ALL THE DETAILS THAT FIT ON A SHEET BEFORE LETTERING. THE PROCEDURE IS SIMILAR TO DRAWING FLOOR PLANS: LIGHT LAYOUT, THEN HEAVIER FOR CLARITY, DIMENSION LINES, LETTERING, FINAL PUNCHING UP OF THE LINE WORK, AND LAST THE HEAVY TITLE.

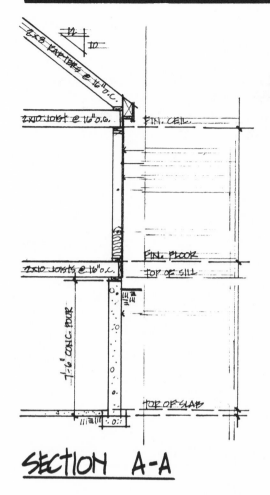

4×8 RAFTERS @ 16" O.C.

12

10

2×10 JOIST @ 16" O.C.

FIN. CEIL.

2×10 JOISTS @ 16" O.C.

FIN. FLOOR

TOP OF SILL

7'-6" CONC. POUR

TOP OF SLAB

SECTION A-A

THE SECTION THROUGH THE BUILDING IS REALLY A LARGE DETAIL AT 3/8" SCALE. YOU CAN'T SHOW MUCH DETAIL AT A SCALE SMALLER THAN THAT, BUT IF THE SECTION IS SIMPLE THEN 1/4" SCALE WILL WORK.

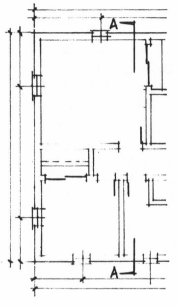

A

A

A

A

THIS IS A NICE SIMPLE WAY TO SHOW WHERE THE SECTION CUTS THROUGH ON THE PLAN.

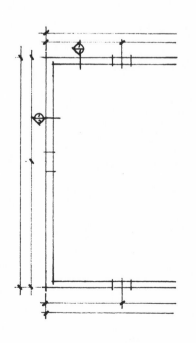

SECTION NUMBER
PAGE SECTION IS ON

THIS SYSTEM IS GOOD IF THERE ARE A LOT OF DRAWINGS. IT MAKES IT EASY TO LOCATE A SPECIFIC DETAIL OR SECTION.

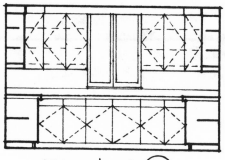

ELEVATION ①

INTERIOR ROOM ELEVATIONS ARE USEFUL, PARTICULAR-LY IN THE KITCHEN AND FIREPLACE WALL. YOU CAN SHOW EXACTLY WHAT IS TO BE BUILT THERE. 1/4" SCALE IS USUAL, BUT A LARGER SIZE IS USED WHEN MORE DETAIL IS REQUIRED.

THE SYSTEM FOR SHOWING THE LOCATION ON THE PLAN IS A CIRCLE ARROW COMBINATION. THE TOP NUMBER IS THE ELEVATION NUMBER AND THE BOTTOM ONE IS THE SHEET THE ELEVATION IS ON.

ELEVATION NUMBER
PAGE ELEVATION IS ON

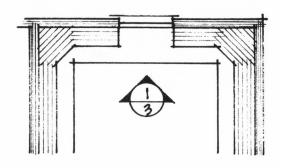

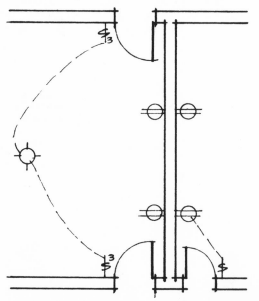

THE ELECTRIC PLAN IS SIMPLE AND USUALLY PUT ON THE FLOOR PLANS. IF THE PLANS ARE VERY "BUSY", A SEPERATE FLOOR PLAN CAN BE TRACED AND THE ELECTICAL LAYOUT DRAWN ON IT.

LIGHT - CEILING

LIGHT - WALL

LIGHT - PULL CHAIN

CONVENIENCE OUTLET

RANGE OUTLET

WATER PROOF OUTLET

$ SWITCH

$₃   3 WAY SWITCH

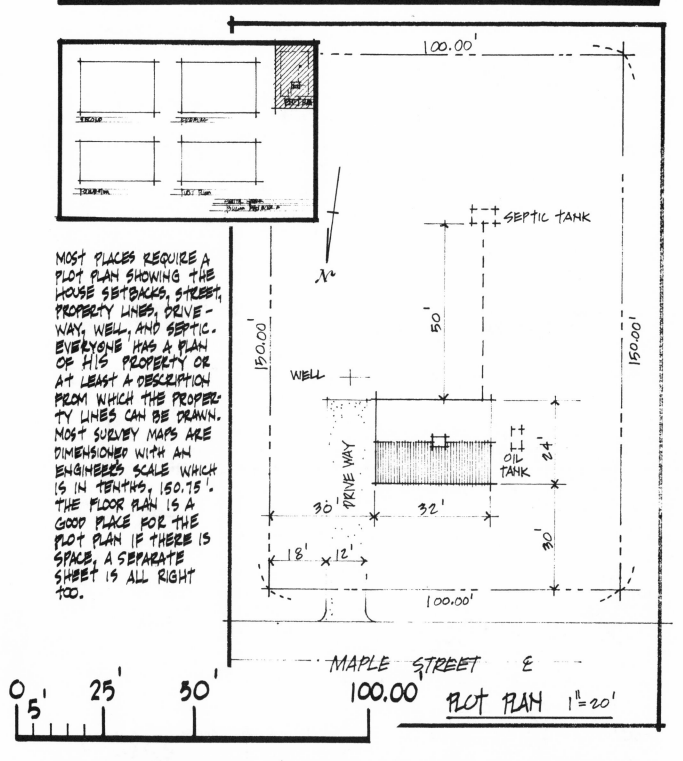

MOST PLACES REQUIRE A PLOT PLAN SHOWING THE HOUSE SETBACKS, STREET, PROPERTY LINES, DRIVEWAY, WELL, AND SEPTIC. EVERYONE HAS A PLAN OF HIS PROPERTY OR AT LEAST A DESCRIPTION FROM WHICH THE PROPERTY LINES CAN BE DRAWN. MOST SURVEY MAPS ARE DIMENSIONED WITH AN ENGINEERS SCALE WHICH IS IN TENTHS, 150.75'. THE FLOOR PLAN IS A GOOD PLACE FOR THE PLOT PLAN IF THERE IS SPACE, A SEPARATE SHEET IS ALL RIGHT TOO.

PLOT PLAN 1"=20'

IF AN ENGINEERS SCALE IS NOT AVAILABLE, MAKE A SCALE USING YOUR SURVEY PLAN. DIVIDE UP SOME DIMENSION UNTIL YOU GET WHAT YOU NEED. DRAW THE PLOT PLAN AT WHATEVER SCALE IS CONVENIENT.

DOOR SCHEDULE

MARK	SIZE	MATERIAL	PATTERN	REMARKS
A	3'-0" x 6'-8 x 1¾"	FIR	108(F-662)	
B	2'-6" x 6'-8" x 1¾"	FIR	L(F-944)	
C	2'-6" x 6'-6" x 1⅜"	PINE	M-1051	
D	2'-4" x 6'-6" x 1⅜"	PINE	M-1051	
E				

THE DOOR SCHEDULE LEAVES NO DOUBT AS TO WHAT IS REQUIRED. IT'S PRETTY TOUGH TO FIT ALL THAT INFORMATION ON THE PLAN.

WITH THE DOOR SCHEDULE THE SYMBOL IS SHOWN ON THE PLAN..

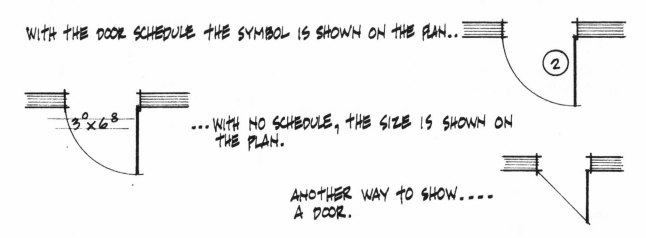

...WITH NO SCHEDULE, THE SIZE IS SHOWN ON THE PLAN.

ANOTHER WAY TO SHOW..... A DOOR.

WINDOW SCHEDULE

MARK	UNIT NO.	AMOUNT REQ.
1	3446	3
2	2042	1
3	C-235	1

THE WINDOW SCHEDULE WORKS LIKE THE DOOR SCHEDULE.

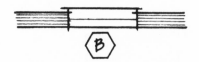

WITH THE SCHEDULE, THE SYMBOL IS SHOWN ON THE PLAN.

WITH NO SCHEDULE, THE UNIT NUMBER IS SHOWN......

ROOM FINISH

ROOM	FLOOR	WALLS	CEILING	BASE	TRIM	REMARKS
ENTRANCE	Vinyl Sheet	½" Sheetrock	½" Sheetrock	Rubber	Pine	
LIVINGROOM	White Oak	½" Sheetrock	½" Sheetrock	1x5	Pine	
DININGROOM	White Oak	½" Sheetrock	½" Sheetrock	1x5	Pine	
KITCHEN	Vinyl Sheet	½" Sheetrock	½" Sheetrock	Rubber	Pine	
BATH #1	Vinyl Sheet	½" Sheetrock	½" Sheetrock	Rubber	Pine	Ceramic tile in tub.

TO AVOID SURPRISING THE BUILDER, A ROOM FINISH SCHEDULE IS A GREAT HELP.

SOME JOBS MIGHT REQUIRE IDENTIFYING EACH WALL IN A ROOM BECAUSE OF MANY DIFFERENT FINISHES. THIS CAN BE DONE WITH THIS SYMBOL ON EVERY FLOOR PLAN, ANY PLACE WILL DO.

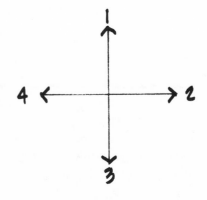

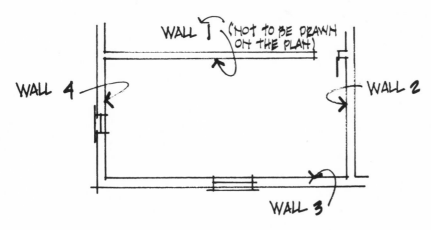

THE ROOM FINISH SCHEDULE WITH THIS SYSTEM WILL SHOW WALL 1, WALL 2, WALL 3, AND WALL 4. THE NUMBER 1 WALL WILL ALWAYS BE THE UPPER, NUMBER 2 THE RIGHT, NUMBER 3 THE BOTTOM, AND NUMBER 4 THE LEFT.

THE LEAD FOR LETTERING SHOULD BE SOFT AND DARK, F OR HB. THE POINT, BEFORE SHARPENING LOOKS LIKE THIS.... NOT UNTIL THE TIP IS SHARPENED BY SANDPAPER OR SHARPENER IS IT READY TO WORK WITH.

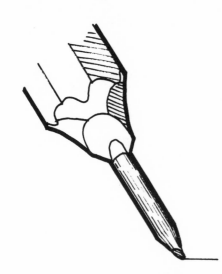

TO GET THIN VERTICAL LINES, ROLL THE PENCIL TO A SHARP CORNER ON THE TIP AND THEN STROKE. FIND THE BROAD PART OF THE TIP FOR THE HORIZONTAL AND CURVED STROKES. THIS COMBINATION MAKES FOR CLEAN CRISP LETTERING.

EXPERIMENT WITH THE TIP; YOU MIGHT LIKE THE CHISEL POINT WHICH IS USED THE SAME WAY, THIN VERTICAL STROKE AND BROAD HORIZONTAL STROKE. MAKE ALL STROKES FROM THE SHOULDER, NOT THE WRIST. USE FIRM SURE VERTICAL STROKES AND QUICK SMOOTH CURVES. THERE IS A LOT OF LETTER-ING ON A PLAN AND SPEED IS A GREAT HELP IN GETTING A JOB DONE, BUT ABOVE ALL, IT MUST BE CLEAR. IF YOU CAN'T READ IT, THE PRETTY IS WORTHLESS. PRACTICE AND DEVELOPE YOUR OWN STYLE. HOLD THE PENCIL WITH A LIGHT TOUCH AND YOU WILL HAVE BETTER CONTROL.

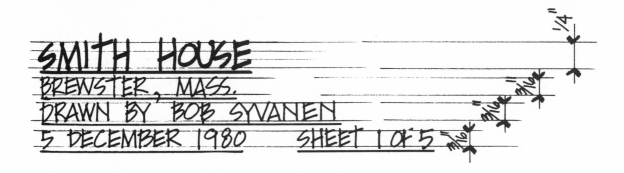

SMITH HOUSE
BREWSTER, MASS.
DRAWN BY BOB SYVANEN
5 DECEMBER 1980   SHEET 1 OF 5

THE TITLES ARE PUT ON ALL THE SHEETS WHEN THE PLANS ARE DONE.

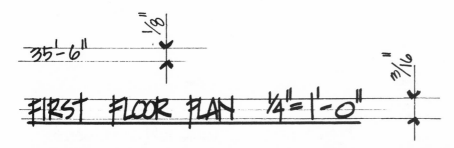

35'-6"

FIRST FLOOR PLAN 1/4"=1'-0"

ALL THESE SIZES SUIT ME. SUIT YOURSELF AND THE SPACE AVAILABLE.

'BED ROOM   1/8" 35'-4"   ON LETTERS AND NUMBERS, LET VERTICAL LINES EXTEND BEYOND GUIDE LINES. MAKE HORIZONTAL AND CURVES RIDE UP. SOME LETTERS CAN RUN TOGETHER.

'BED ROOM   35'-4"   YOU GET A HANG DOG-LOOK WHEN VERTICAL LINES SLANT AND HORIZONTAL LINES DROOP.

| | | QUICK FIRM VERTICAL STROKES.

3 ⊂ C D D   QUICK SMOOTH CURVES.

LET THE GUIDE LINES SHOW ON THE PRINTS, I THINK THEY HELP THE LOOKS OF THE LETTERING. KEEP THEM THIN SO THEY DON'T CONFLICT WITH DIMENSION LINES.

73

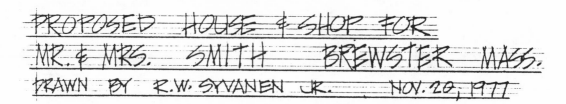

PROPOSED HOUSE & SHOP FOR
MR. & MRS. SMITH BREWSTER MASS.
DRAWN BY R.W. SYVANEN JR. NOV. 20, 1977

THIS IS MY STYLE FOR FAST LETTERING. I USED THREE LINES.

PROPOSED ADDITION FOR PHIL TARVERS
BREWSTER, MASS. DRAWN BY BOB SYVANEN 23 APR. 1980

YOU CAN DO THE SAME THING ON TWO LINES.

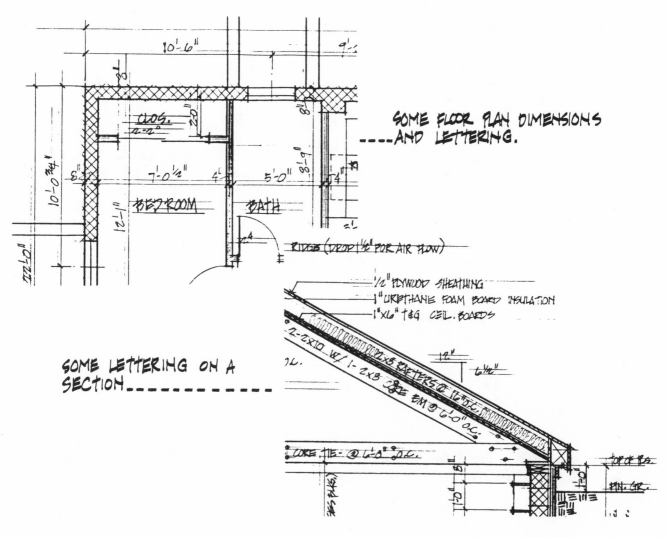

SOME FLOOR PLAN DIMENSIONS
----AND LETTERING.

SOME LETTERING ON A
SECTION-------------

WOOD BLOCKING

WOOD TIMBER

FINISH WOOD OR TRIM

PLYWOOD

CONCRETE BLOCK

POURED CONCRETE

SAND

FIBERGLASS INSULATION

RIGID INSULATION

FOAM BOARD

BRICK (SECTION)

THESE ARE THE MOST COMMON SYMBOLS.

DRAFTING

———————/——————— BROKEN LINE OR SECTION

——— · ——— · ⊄ ——— CENTER LINE

— — — — — — — — BURIED OR HIDDEN LINE

━━━ ━ ━ ━━━ ━ ━ ━━━ BEAM

———————————— GUIDE LINES

———————————— DIMENSION LINES

━━━━━━━━━━━━ HEAVY OUTLINE

FINISHED GRADE
EARTH

GRAVEL

ABBREVIATIONS THESE ABBREVIATIONS ARE ALWAYS USED. TRY TO SPELL ALL OTHER WORDS FOR CLARITY.

O.C. — ON CENTER — 16" O.C.   ⊄ —— CENTER LINE ——·⊄·——

& — AND — SAND & GRAVEL   W/ —— WITH — ½" W/ PLYWOOD OVER

@ — AT — 2x4 STUDS @ 16" O.C.   CONC. —— CONCRETE

76

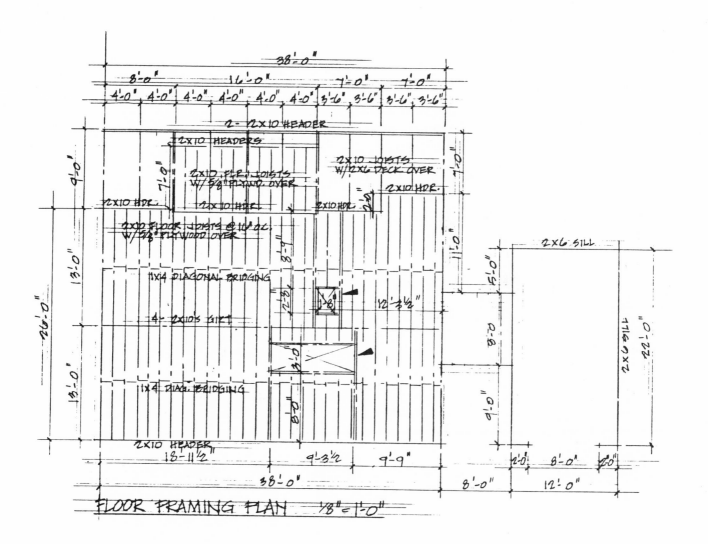

FLOOR FRAMING PLAN   ⅛"=1'-0"

FLOOR FRAMING PLANS CAN BE AT ANY SCALE FROM ¹/₁₆"=1'-0" TO ¼"=1'-0".
THIS PLAN WORKED WELL FOR ME AT ⅛"=1'-0". WHERE CHIMNEY AND STAIRS
ARE, X THEM TO SHOW THERE IS NO FRAMING.

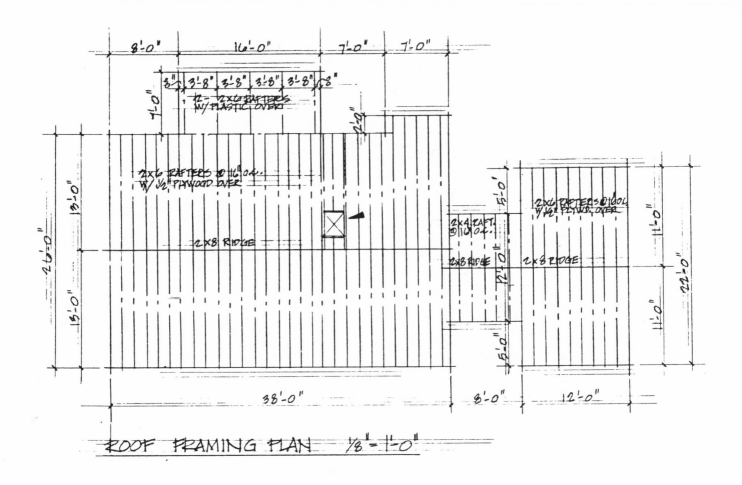

ROOF FRAMING PLAN   1/8" = 1'-0"

THIS ROOF FRAMING PLAN IS FROM THE SAME SET OF PLANS. AGAIN, X WHERE THERE IS AN OPENING. IN THIS CASE IT IS THE CHIMNEY.

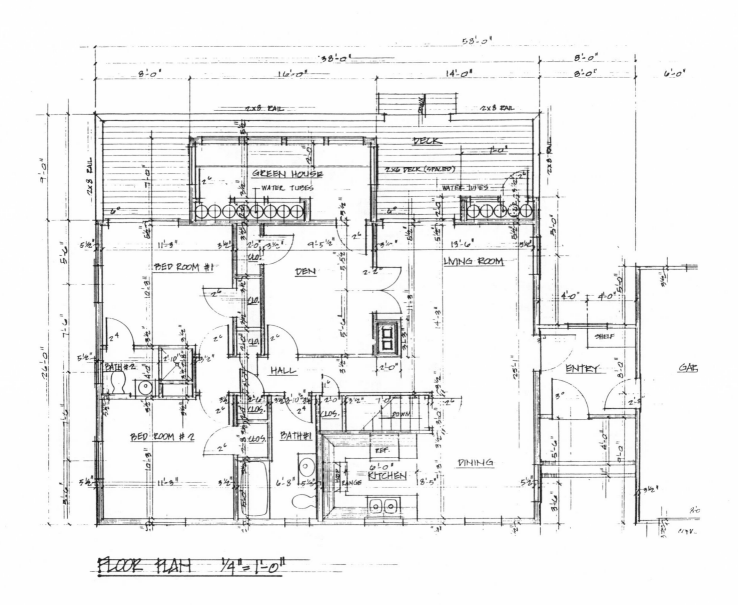

FLOOR PLAN ¼"=1'-0"

THIS FLOOR PLAN IS TYPICAL. IT SHOWS ALL THAT IS NECESSARY FOR CONSTRUCTION. THE ROOF AND FLOOR FRAMING PLANS ARE FROM THIS PLAN.

CONDITION @ CORNER

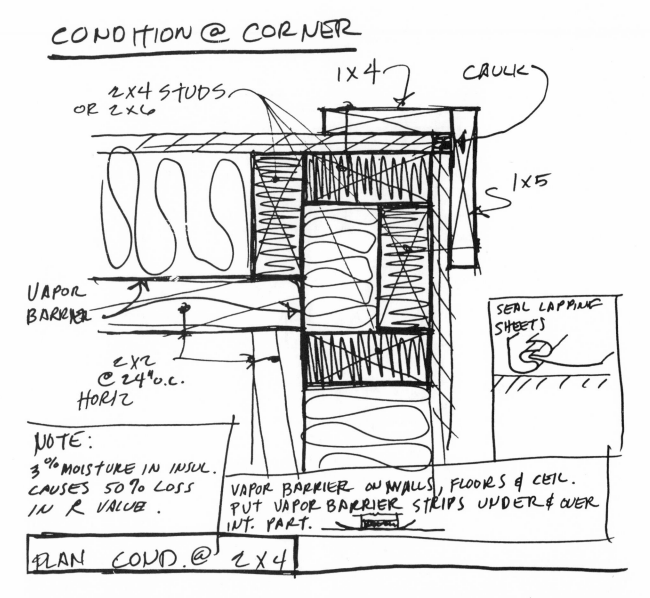

2×4 STUDS.
OR 2×6

1X4

CAULK

1X5

VAPOR BARRIER

SEAL LAPPING SHEETS

2×2 @ 24" O.C. HORIZ

NOTE:
3% MOISTURE IN INSUL. CAUSES 50% LOSS IN R VALUE.

VAPOR BARRIER ON WALLS, FLOORS & CEIL. PUT VAPOR BARRIER STRIPS UNDER & OVER INT. PART.

PLAN COND. @ 2×4

DETAILS CAN BE AS SIMPLE AS THIS TO GET THE JOB DONE. THIS IS WHAT THE CARPENTER DOES ON THE JOB IF THE DETAILS ARE NOT ON THE PLANS. IF YOU WANT THE JOB DONE YOUR WAY IT IS BEST TO DRAW IT FIRST. THIS IS A PLAN OF AN OUTSIDE CORNER FOR A SCANDANIVIAN WALL. THERE IS GOOD NAILING FOR CORNER BOARDS AND ACCESS TO INSULATE THE CORNER FROM INSIDE THE BUILDING. THIS MAKES A NICE TIGHT DRAFT-FREE CORNER.

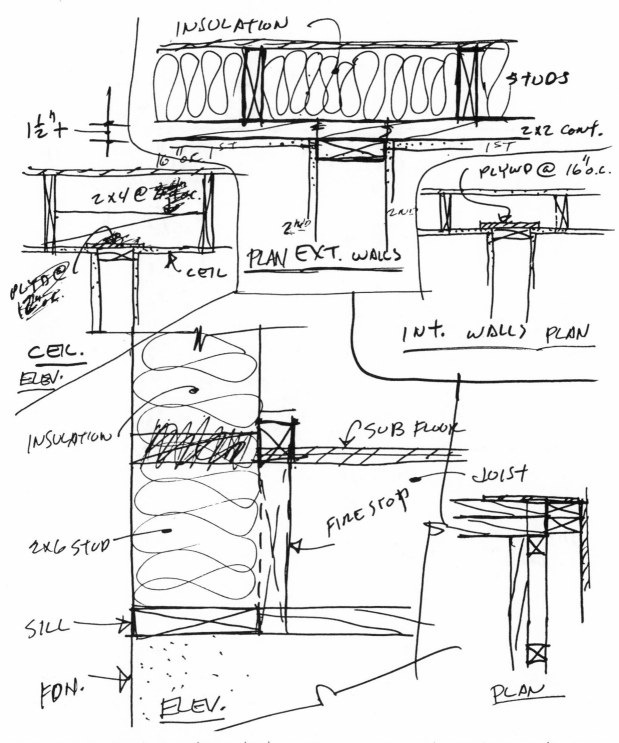

INSULATION

STUDS

$1\frac{1}{2}"+$

2×2 cont.

16"o.c. 1ST

1ST

2×4 @ 16"o.c.

PLYWD @ 16"o.c.

PLYWD @ FLOOR

CEIL

2ND

2ND

PLAN EXT. WALLS

INT. WALLS PLAN

CEIL.
ELEV.

INSULATION

SUB FLOOR

JOIST

2×6 STUD

FIRE STOP

SILL

FDN.

ELEV.

PLAN

MORE QUICK SKETCH DETAILS THAT WORK, BUT ARE NOT ALWAYS CLEAR TO OTHERS
USE FELT TIP PEN OR SOFT PENCIL.

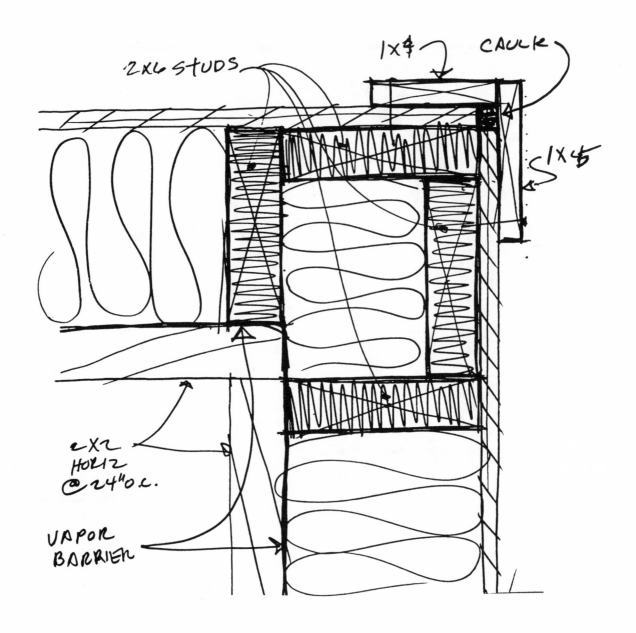

THE SAME SCANDINAVIAN WALL DETAIL WITH 2X6 STUDS. ALL THESE QUICK SKETCH DETAILS CAN BE USED AS IS AND XEROX COPIES MADE TO PASS AROUND.

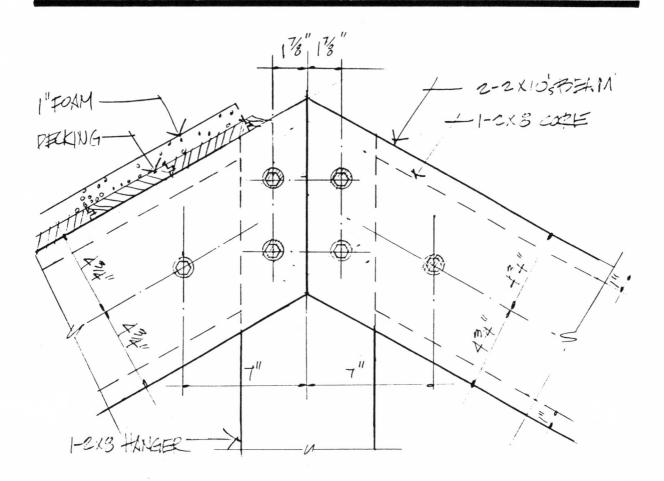

1" FOAM

DECKING

1 7/8" 1 7/8"

2-2X10's BEAM

1-2X8 CORE

4 3/4"

4 3/4"

7" 7"

1-2X8 HANGER

BEAM & HANGER @ RIDGE

3" = 1'-0"

WHEN A LITTLE MORE PRECISION IS REQUIRED, I GO TO THIS SYSTEM. AT THIS SCALE, THINGS CAN BE MEASURED OFF EASILY.

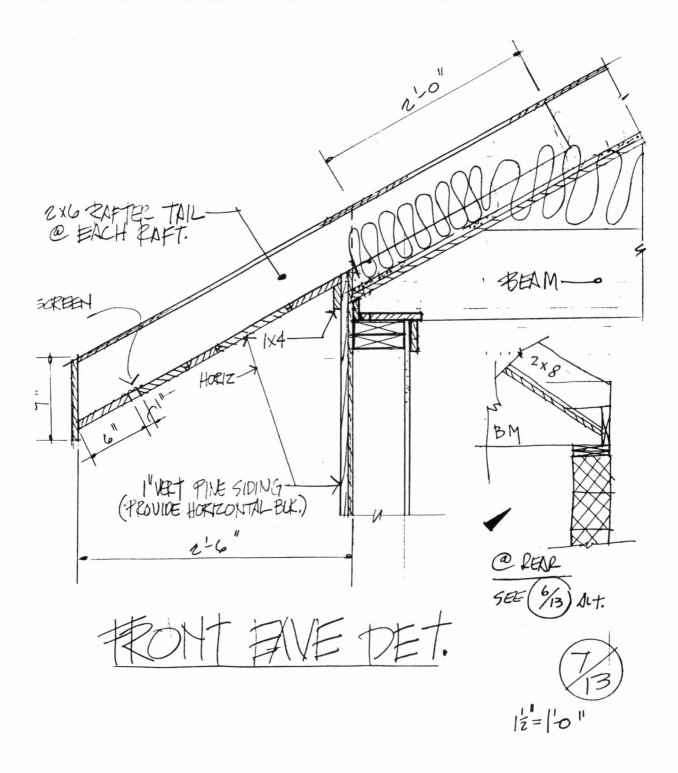

2X6 RAFTER TAIL @ EACH RAFT.

SCREEN

2'-0"

BEAM

1X4

HORIZ

7"

6"

6"

1" VERT PINE SIDING (PROVIDE HORIZONTAL BLK.)

2'-6"

2 X 8

BM

@ REAR

SEE ⑥/₁₃ ALT.

⑦/₁₃

$1\frac{1}{2}" = 1'-0"$

FRONT EAVE DET.

WHAT IS DRAWN DOESN'T ALWAYS WORK BEST AND A REVISION TAKES PLACE IN THE FIELD.

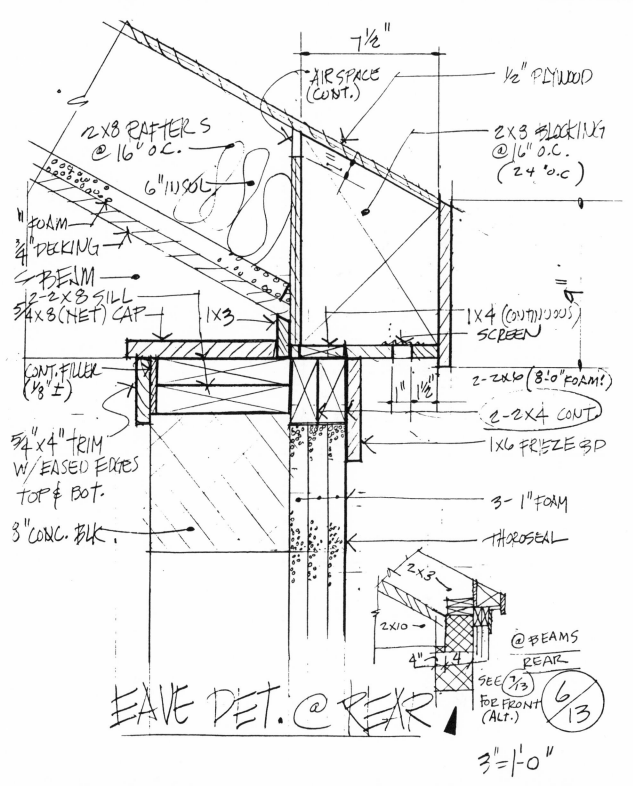

7½"

AIR SPACE (CONT.)

½" PLYWOOD

2X8 RAFTERS @ 16" O.C.

2X3 BLOCKING @ 16" O.C. (24" O.C.)

6" INSOL

FOAM

¾" DECKING

BEAM

2-2X8 SILL
5/4X8 (NET) CAP

1X3

1X4 (CONTINUOUS) SCREEN

CONT. FILLER (⅛" ±)

1" 1½"

2-2X6 (8'-0" FOAM!)

2-2X4 CONT.

5/4"X4" TRIM W/EASED EDGES TOP & BOT.

1X6 FRIEZE BD

3- 1" FOAM

3" CONC. BLK.

THOROSEAL

EAVE DET. @ REAR

2X3

2X10

4" 4"

@ BEAMS
REAR

SEE 7/13
FOR FRONT
(ALT.)

6/13

3"=1'-0"

ONCE AGAIN YOU THINK YOU HAVE IT ALL FIGURED, BUT AT LEAST THERE IS A PLACE TO START FROM.

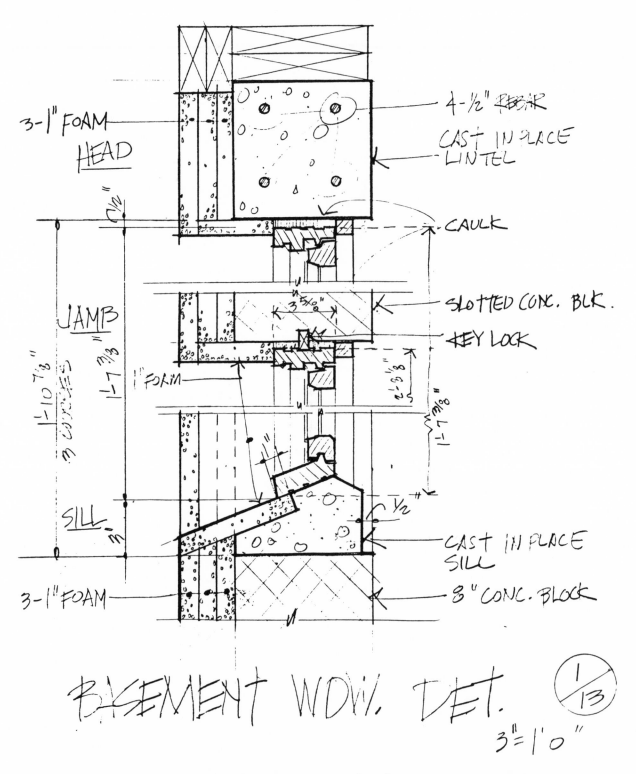

3-1" FOAM
HEAD

4-½" REBAR

CAST IN PLACE
LINTEL

CAULK

JAMB

SLOTTED CONC. BLK.

KEY LOCK

1" FORM

SILL

CAST IN PLACE
SILL

3-1" FOAM

8" CONC. BLOCK

BASEMENT WDW. DET. ①/13

3"=1'0"

ALL THESE DETAILS WERE DRAWN ON 8½"x11" SHEETS, IN PENCIL, AND
XEROX COPIES MADE FOR USE ON THE JOB.

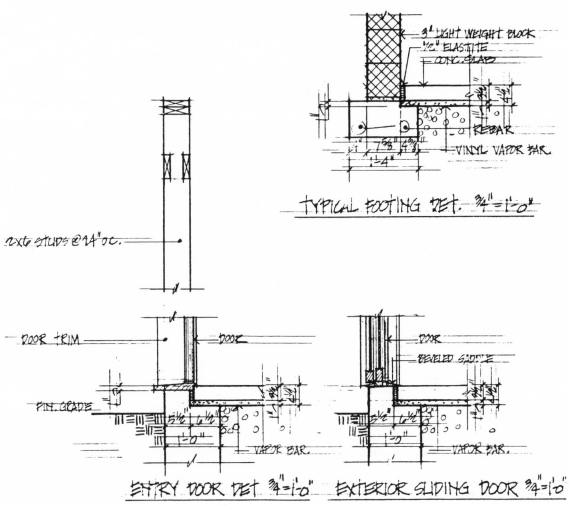

TYPICAL FOOTING DET. ¾"=1'-0"

3" LIGHT WEIGHT BLOCK
½" ELASTITE
CONC. SLAB
REBAR
VINYL VAPOR BAR.

2x6 STUDS @ 24" O.C.

DOOR TRIM
DOOR
FIN. GRADE
VAPOR BAR.

ENTRY DOOR DET ¾"=1'-0"

DOOR
BEVELED SADDLE
VAPOR BAR.

EXTERIOR SLIDING DOOR ¾"=1'-0"

FROM BOTH ROUGH AND REFINED SKETCHES, THESE DETAIL DRAWING WERE MADE ON THE PLANS. PLANS WILL READ BETTER IF ALL RELATED DETAILS LIKE FOUNDATION DETAILS OR WINDOW DETAILS, ARE KEPT TOGETHER.

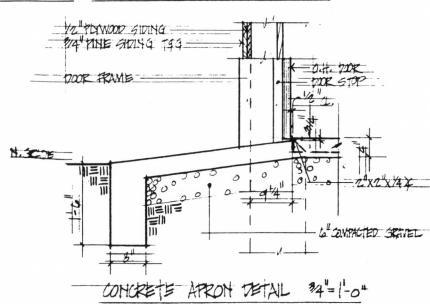

½" PLYWOOD SIDING
¾" PINE SIDING T&G
DOOR FRAME
FIN. GRADE
O.H. DOOR
DOOR STOP
2"x2"x¼"
6" COMPACTED GRAVEL

CONCRETE APRON DETAIL ¾"=1'-0"

PERSPECTIVES CAN BE A GREAT HELP IN VISUALIZING THE FINISHED PRODUCT. THEY CAN BE PLAIN OR FANCY. THERE IS A LOT WRITTEN ON THIS SUBJECT AND IN FACT MOST ARCHITECTURAL FIRMS FARM THIS WORK OUT.

ELEVATION "A" EXISTING BUILDING — TEXTURE 1-11 PLYWOOD SIDING

YOU MIGHT TRY SIMPLE WORK LIKE THIS THAT I DID FOR A REMODEL JOB.

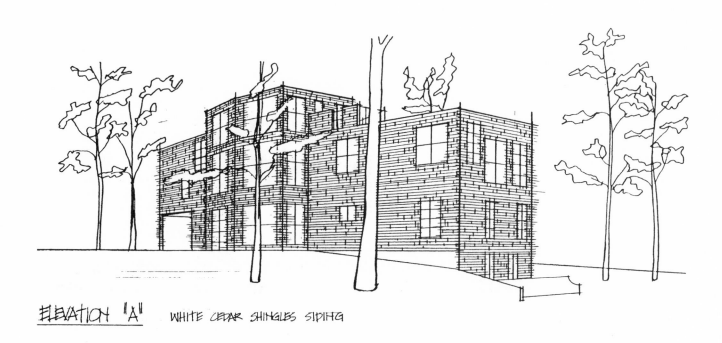

ELEVATION "A"   WHITE CEDAR SHINGLES SIDING

I USED SIMPLE PERSPECTIVE TECHNIQUES, THE OLD "VANISHING POINTS" WE ALL
LEARNED ABOUT IN HIGH SCHOOL.

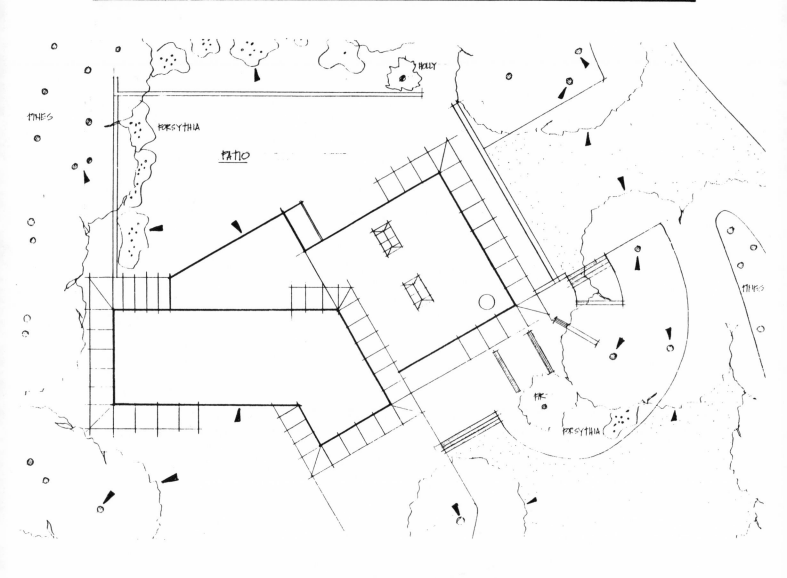

THIS LANDSPAPE PLAN SHOWS THE ROOF AND SURROUNDING FOLIAGE. THE TREE TRUNKS ARE LOCATED AND THEN THE SHAPES ARE SIMULATED AROUND THEM.

A SMALL HOUSE IS USUALLY EASY TO DRAW, BUT NOT ALWAYS EASY TO DESIGN. WITH A LARGE HOUSE THERE ARE ALL TYPES OF SPACE TO WORK WITH— STAIRWAYS, KITCHEN APPLIANCES, TUBS, AND SINKS WILL FIT ANYWHERE. A SMALL HOUSE IS LIMITED AND CLEVER DESIGN IS NECESSARY.

THE FOLLOWING PAGES SHOW A SMALL PASSIVE SOLAR HOUSE THAT WORKED WELL. AS WITH ANY HOUSE, THE OWNERS MADE CHANGES THEY WISH THEY HADN'T, AND THOUGHT OF THINGS THEY SHOULD HAVE DONE. I DON'T KNOW OF ANYONE WHO HAS BUILT THE "PERFECT HOUSE". THERE ARE ALWAYS THINGS THAT SHOULD HAVE BEEN DONE DIFFERENTLY.

SKYLIGHTS ARE GREAT, BUT THEY HAVE A TENDENCY TO LEAK, ARE DIFFICULT TO SHADE IN SUMMER, AND LOOSE MUCH HEAT IN WINTER. A WELL BUILT SKYLIGHT, PROPERLY INSTALLED, SHOULD NOT LEAK. MOTHER NATURE, WITH A TALL LEAFY TREE, OR ANY OTHER WELL DESIGNED SUN SCREEN, WILL TAKE CARE OF THE SUMMER SUN. INSULATING PANELS OR DRAPES (THE SIMPLER THE BETTER) WILL KEEP THE WINTER HEAT IN.

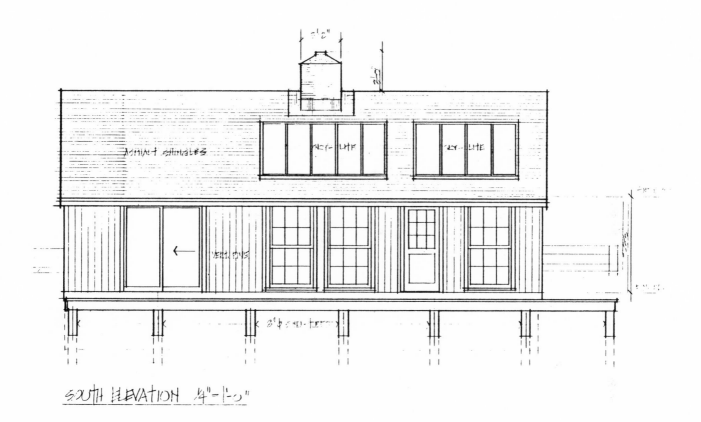

SOUTH ELEVATION ¼"=1'-0"

THEY DON'T ALWAYS TURN OUT THE SAME AS THE PLANS.

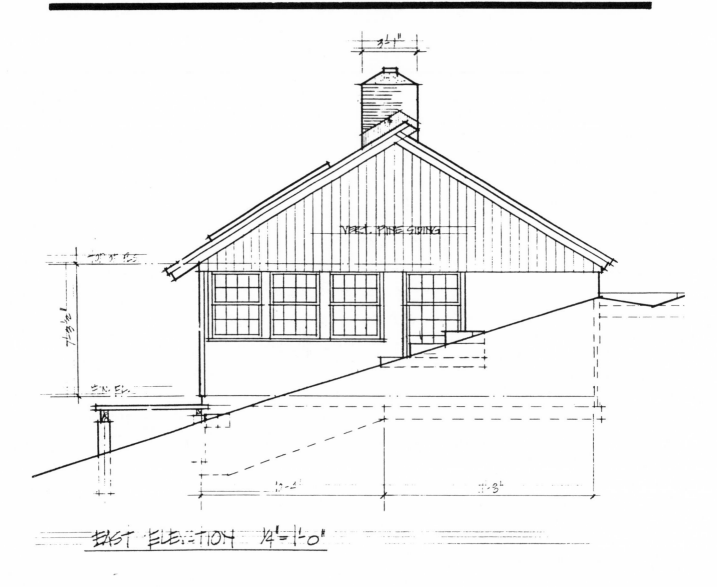

EAST ELEVATION 1/4"=1'-0"

THE HOUSE WASN'T BUILT ON THE ORIGINAL LOCATION AND THAT'S WHY THE DIFFERENCE IN GROUND SLOPE. IT WORKED BETTER THIS WAY.

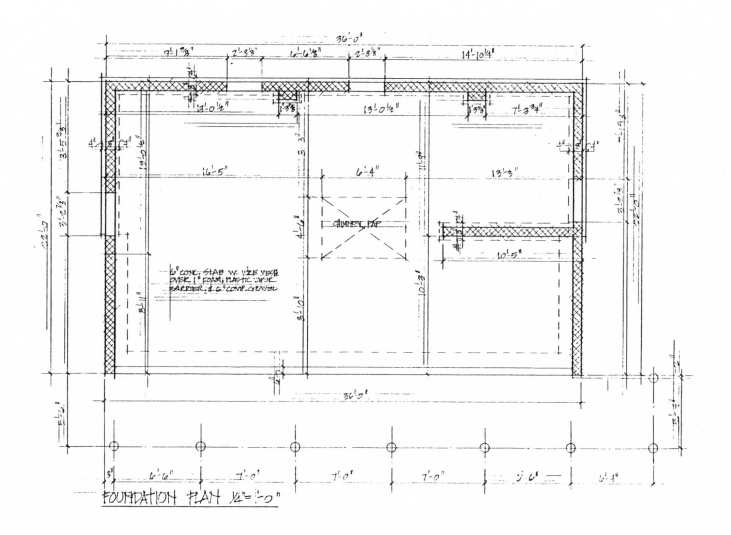

FOUNDATION PLAN ¼"=1'-0"

THE FOUNDATION WAS TO BE CONCRETE BLOCK, BUT POURED CONCRETE WAS USED TO SAVE TIME.

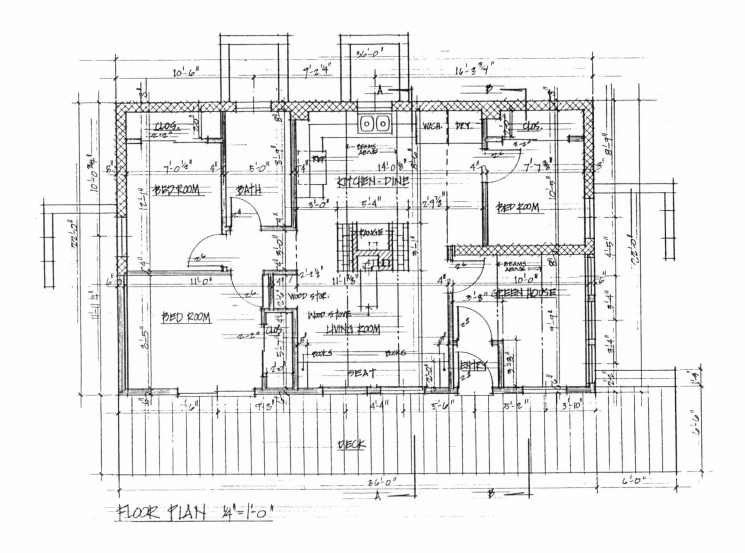

FLOOR PLAN ¼"=1'-0"

IT WAS A SIMPLE FLOOR PLAN THAT WAS EASY TO DRAW. THE AIR-LOCK ENTRY WAS NOT BUILT; THEY WISH THEY HAD.

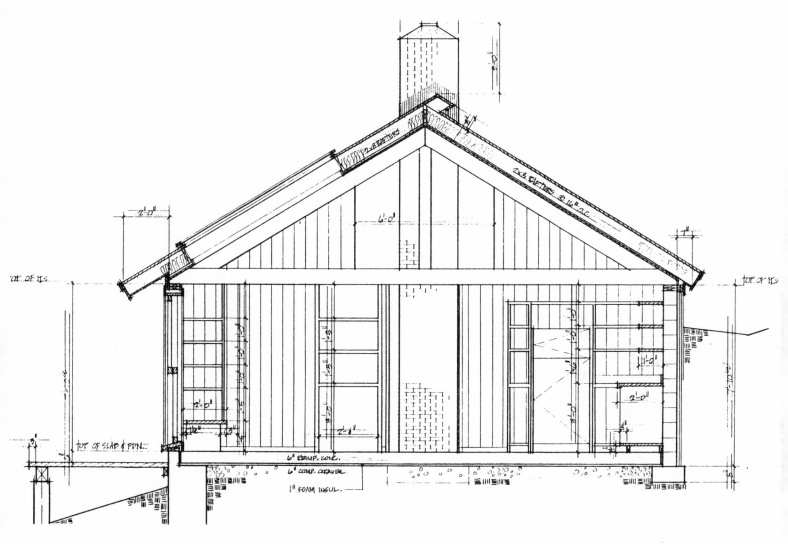

SECTION A-A   3/8" = 1'-0"

A SECTION THROUGH THE BUILDING SHOWING ALL THAT YOU WOULD SEE IF LOOKING
IN THAT DIRECTION. THE FLOOR PLAN SHOWS WHERE IT CUTS THROUGH. THE
FOAM INSULATION UNDER THE CONCRETE SLAB FLOOR SHOULD BE UNDER THE GRAVEL
AND ON TOP OF A VAPOR BARRIER. THE GRAVEL WOULD THEN STORE HEAT WITH
THE FLOOR SLAB.

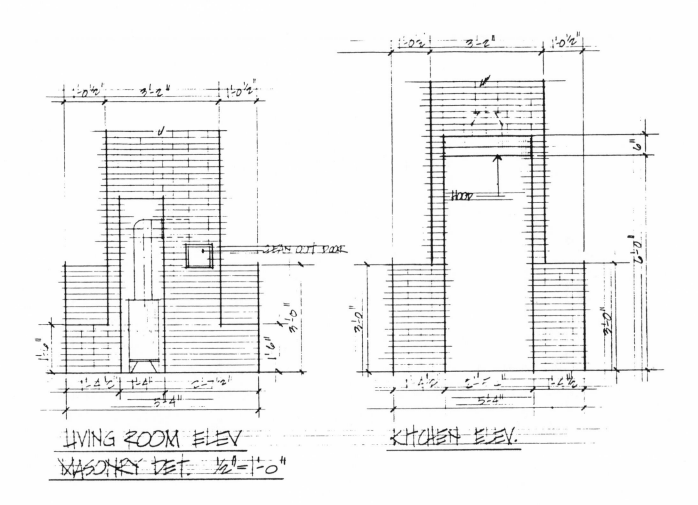

LIVING ROOM ELEV.

MASONRY DET. ½"=1'-0"

KITCHEN ELEV.

THIS MASONRY UNIT WAS NOT BUILT EITHER. THEY OPTED FOR A FIREPLACE WHICH
TURNED OUT VERY NICE. FIREPLACES ARE NOT VERY ENERGY EFFICIENT, BUT
THEY CAN BE GOOD HEAT RADIATORS IF THE RUMFORD STYLE IS USED. THE RUM-
FORD STYLE OPENING IS WIDE AND HIGH (ABOUT AS HIGH AS IT IS WIDE), WITH
A SHALLOW HEARTH. THERE IS A GOOD PAPER BACK BOOK ABOUT THIS FIREPLACE.

MOST SMALL HOUSES ARE LOW BUDGET HOUSES WHICH ADD TO THE DE-SIGN DIFFICULTY. THE FOLLOWING HOUSE-SHOP DESIGN WAS NO EXCEPTION.

THE OWNERS WANTED THREE THINGS, A SHOP WITH AN OLD LOOK, PASSIVE SOLAR LIVING QUARTERS, AND A WARM LOOK IN THE CONCRETE LIVING QUARTERS. THE OLD LOOK IS ACCOMPLISHED WITH UNPAINTED PINE SIDING, LOTS OF GLASS ON THE SOUTH, TWO TROMBE WALLS, AND A GREENHOUSE WHICH GIVE THIS HOUSE TREMENDOUS HEATING POTENTIAL. THE LIVING ROOM, DINING AND KITCHEN AREA HAS 4x6 ADZED BEAMS WITH A WOOD CEILING TO GIVE IT A WARM LOOK.

THE PORCH ON THE SHOP ENTRANCE SIDE IS INVITING. THE SKYLIGHT
NEEDS SHADING.

THIS IS AN EXAMPLE OF A SIMPLE, QUICK PERSPECTIVE AND SINCE I BUILT THE HOUSE, THE FINISHED PRODUCT IS PRETTY MUCH THE SAME.

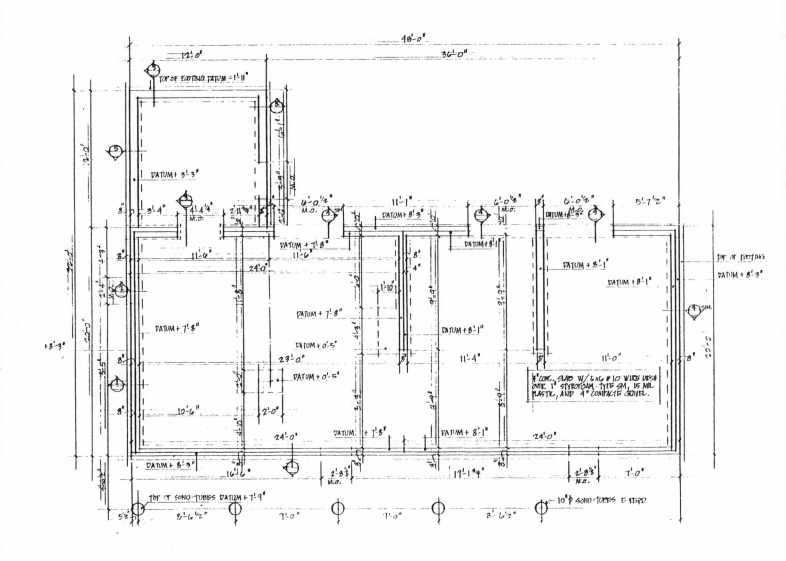

I HAD A LOT OF DIFFERENT CONCRETE HEIGHTS SO I CALLED THEM OUT AS DATUM
+ 8'-1" OR DATUM + 8'-3". THE CONCRETE CONTRACTOR FOUND IT TOO MUCH TROUBLE
SO I MADE SOME CHANGES. THE SIMPLER THE PLANS ARE THE FEWER PROBLEMS
YOU WILL ENCOUNTER.

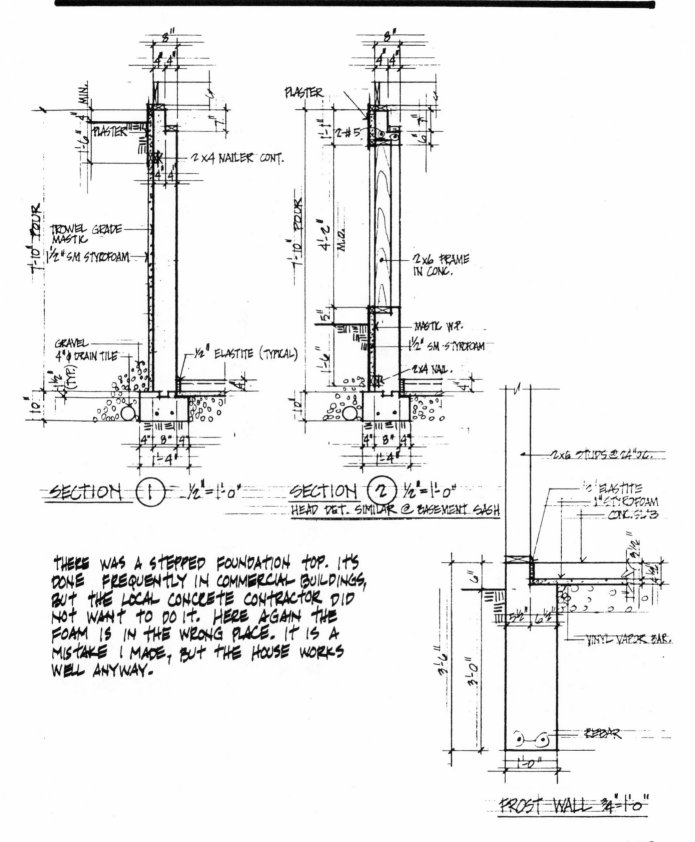

SECTION ① ½"=1'-0"

SECTION ② ½"=1'-0"
HEAD DET. SIMILAR @ BASEMENT SASH

FROST WALL ¾"=1'-0"

THERE WAS A STEPPED FOUNDATION TOP. IT'S
DONE FREQUENTLY IN COMMERCIAL BUILDINGS,
BUT THE LOCAL CONCRETE CONTRACTOR DID
NOT WANT TO DO IT. HERE AGAIN THE
FOAM IS IN THE WRONG PLACE. IT IS A
MISTAKE I MADE, BUT THE HOUSE WORKS
WELL ANYWAY.

103

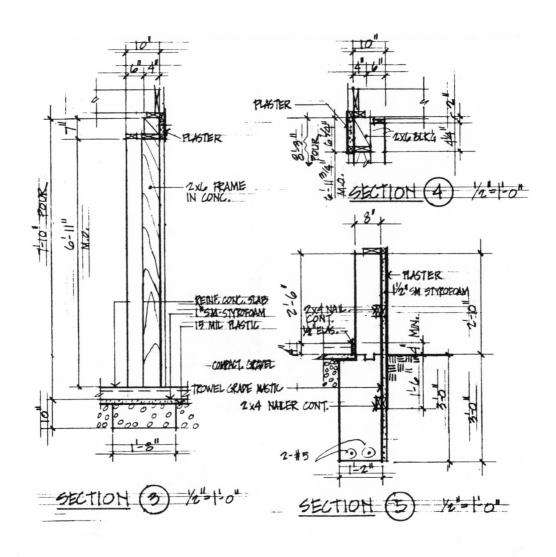

SECTION ③ ½"=1'-0"

SECTION ④ ½"=1'-0"

SECTION ⑤ ½"=1'-0"

THESE DETAILS WERE DRAWN ON THE SHEET WITH THE FOUNDATION PLANS, IT's EASIER TO READ THAT WAY. AS YOU LOOK AROUND YOU WILL FIND MANY WAYS TO DO THE SAME JOB AND JUST BECAUSE IT HASN'T BEEN DONE THAT WAY BEFORE DOESN'T MEAN IT'S WRONG.

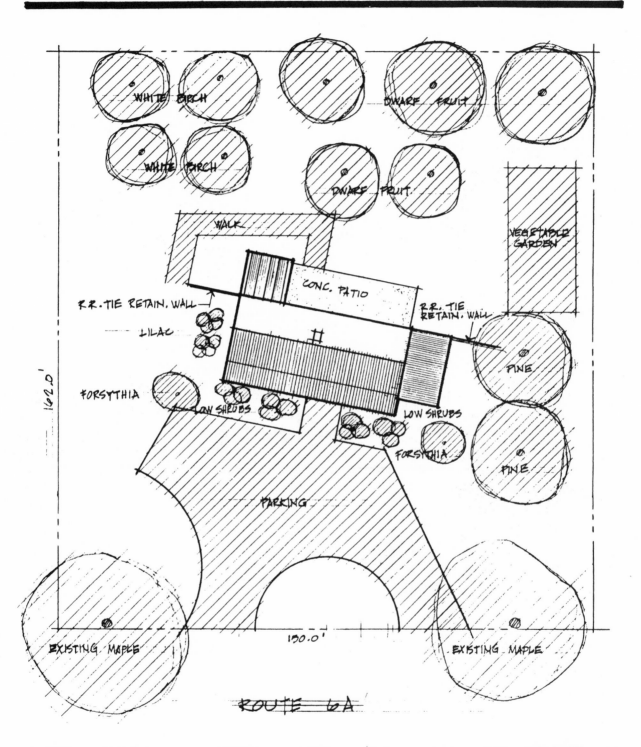

ROUTE 6A

ANOTHER EXAMPLE OF A LANDSCAPE PLOT PLAN. THIS PLAN WAS DONE BECAUSE OF A LOCAL REGULATION. THAT'S WHAT THEY WANTED SO THAT'S WHAT WE GAVE THEM.

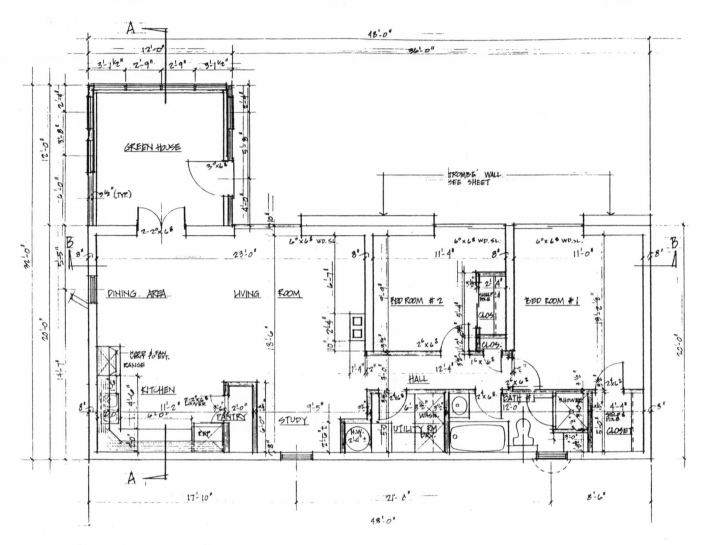

FLOOR PLAN 1/4" = 1'-0"

ANOTHER SIMPLE FLOOR PLAN. I HAVE FOUND THAT THE EASIER IT IS TO DRAW, THE
EASIER IT IS TO BUILD.

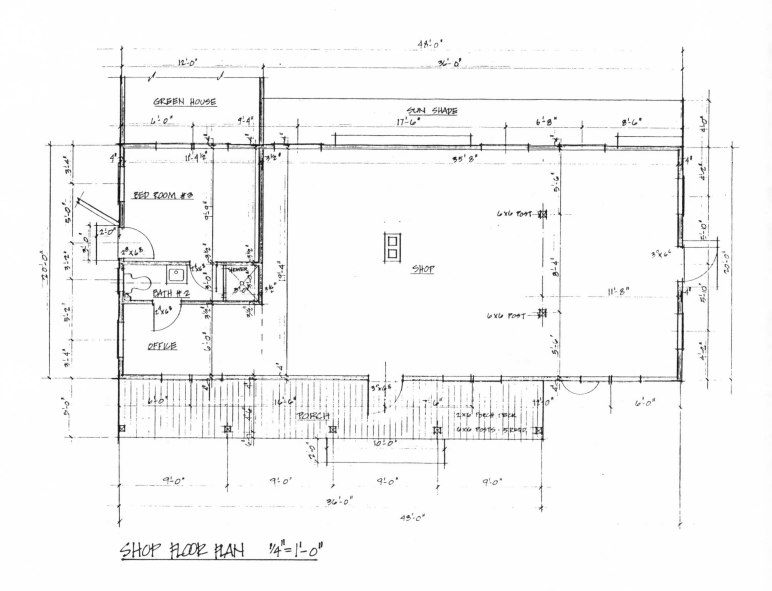

SHOP FLOOR PLAN 1/4"=1'-0"

I CUT OFF THE GREENHOUSE ON THIS DRAWING BECAUSE I NEEDED THE SPACE.

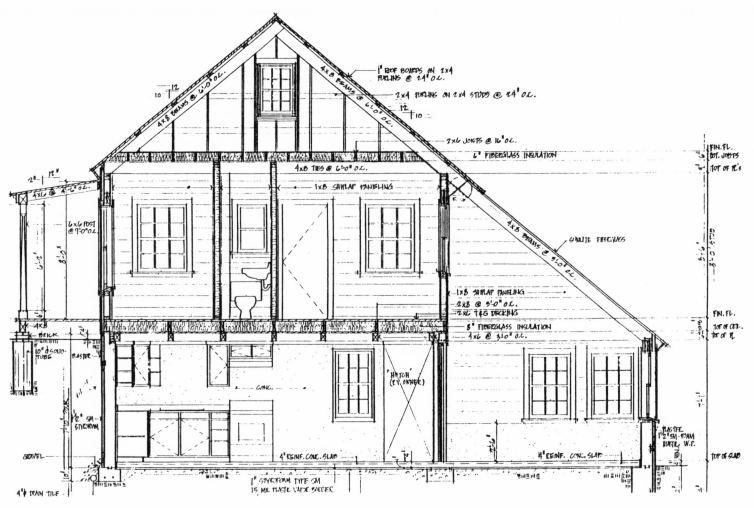

SECTION A-A   3/8" = 1'-0"

A SECTION THROUGH THE MAIN HOUSE AND GREEN HOUSE. THE FOAM INSULATION
IS WRONG HERE TOO.

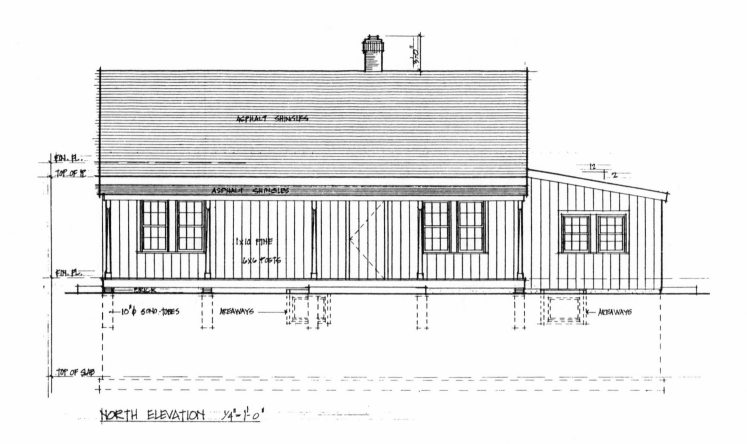

NORTH ELEVATION 1/4"=1'-0"

A VERY SIMPLE BUILDING WITH VERY SIMPLE ELEVATIONS.

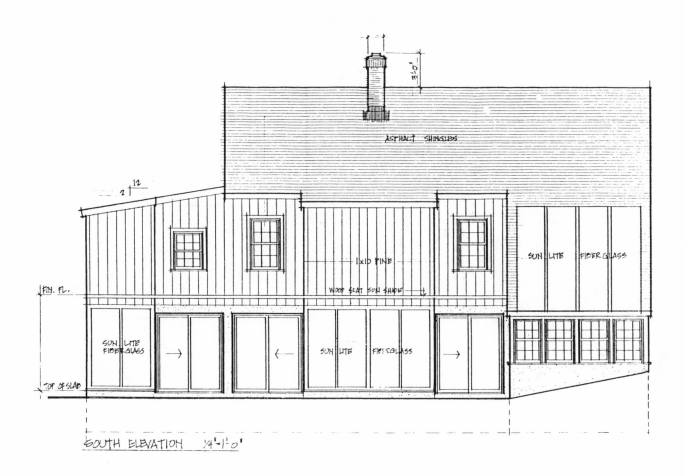

ASPHALT SHINGLES

2 | 12

1X10 PINE

WOOD SLAT SUN SHADE

SUN LITE FIBER GLASS

FIN. FL.

SUN LITE FIBER GLASS

SUN LITE FIBER GLASS

TOP OF SLAB

SOUTH ELEVATION ¼"=1'-0"

A LITTLE MORE COMPLEX ON THE SOUTH SIDE.

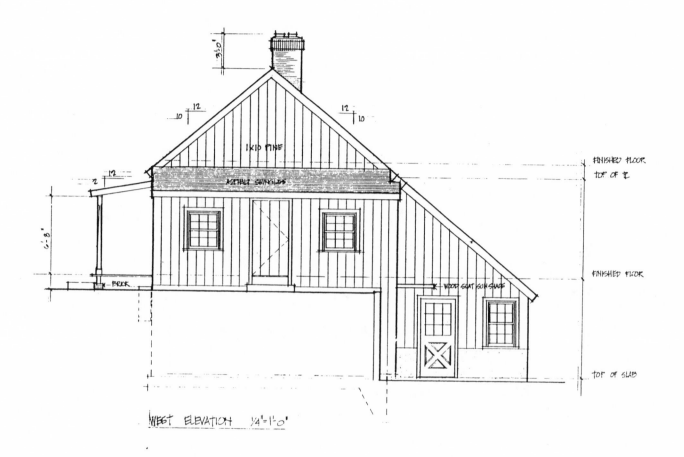

WEST ELEVATION ¼"=1'-0"

THIS ELEVATION SHOWS UP THE DIFFERENT GROUND LEVELS AS WELL AS THE FOUNDATION CONDITIONS.

ALSO OF INTEREST FROM THE GLOBE PEQUOT PRESS:

CARPENTRY: SOME TRICKS OF THE TRADE

INTERIOR FINISH: MORE TRICKS OF THE TRADE

HOW TO AFFORD YOUR OWN LOG HOME